Conversation Guide

ENGLISH-SPANISH

D0892579

© 2001, Editorial LIBSA
C/ San Rafael, 4
28108 Alcobendas (Madrid)
Tel.: 91 657 25 80
Fax: 91 657 25 83
e-mail: libsa@libsa.es
www.libsa.es

ISBN: 84-8238-307-8
Depósito Legal: M-1837-01

Impreso en España/*Printed in Spain*

Index

Introduction

Esteemed reader:

You have in your hands a small manual that can be a big help to you. For that reason we want to inform you of its usefulness: We try to assist the traveller in everyday situations that might occur during their trip. We do this by providing you with groups of guide phrases and a working vocabulary for each of those situations. In that way the user of this guide will be able to make himself understood by correctly using the language of the country in which he finds himself, with the added benefit that this effort counts in the acceptance that one receives and the fluidity of the relationships that one strikes up during his travels

The guide is structured by sections that correspond with generic situations that frequently present themselves to us in our foreign travels.

In each section we will find a group of standard phrases of the native language that will permit us a practical and easy use of it. That is accompanied by a basic vocabulary that will amplify your conversational possibilities and will be useful aid in your travels.

Each phrase or word example in Spanish is followed by it's corresponding translation which is highlighted in *italics,* along with a figurative pronunciation expressed in italics of a smaller size.

We believe that this figurative pronunciation will be extremely useful to you. To make it easier for you we have avoided the technical phonetic system of symbols or, what other guides of this nature do, which is overwhelm the reader with preliminary instructions that are impossible to memorize.

Our guide presents you with a system of pronunciation based exclusively on the spanish alphabet and it´s phonetics. The user should pronounce the words in italics as if he was reading spanish.

This will confirm that the person you are speaking to understands you with no problems. We are aware that not all sounds can be transcribed in their total purity through spanish orthography and phonetics, nevertheless, we are sure that the advantages of our basic system, which avoids the use of complicated symbols, will amply compensate for the inconvenience of small deviations that, in actuality could occur between the native speakers themselves.

In addition, the user of this guide will find, at the beginning of it, some essential elements of grammar and pronunciation. Nonetheless, we want to clarify that it is not the purpose of this guide to offer a language course, but rather to function as an aid for practical usage. Utilized in that way, we believe that its consultation can be helpful for some essential aspects of verb conjugation or the correspondence of an article with the noun it accompanies.

Finally, we would like to stress that by including a thematic vocabulary in structured sections throughout the guide, instead of an appendix dictionary at the end , will faciltate you in finding the appropriate phrase or word for the situations you find yourself in during your travels to foreign countries. For example, if you find yourself in a store and you´d like to buy a certain object, you only have to substitute the word given in the guide section entitled shopping for the desired one. The vocabulary lists are found at the end of each particular section.

In short, we try to help you cross those small barriers that one might encounter upon undertaking the speaking of spanish.

Figurative: Pronunciation

Spanish pronunciation is not difficult and does not present irregularities. Our system of pronunciation is based on the comparison between sounds... and Spanish sounds.

Being conscious of the lack of exactitude of this system, we have chosen in order to give you a simple manuel within everyone´s reach.

Following that, we offer you some observations that will make the pronunciation of this language easier for you.

Vowels: in Spanish nasal vowel sounds do not exist. So, we will eliminate the nasality of syllables....

E is always pronounced like... ay

U is pronounced...oo. It is silent in the syllables "que, qui, gue,gui"

(except when it wields a diaeresis ü: cigüeña, vergüenza.

Consonants

C is pronounced K. Before E and O like the in thin

Ch is pronounced CH

G is pronounced kh before E and I

or like G in go

H is never pronounced

J is pronounced kh

LL is pronounced y

ñ is pronounced ny

R is thrilled

RR is strongly thrilled

S is pronounced like S in sit

V is pronounced bh

Y is pronounced Y

Z is pronounced Th

Note: All of the consonants at the end of the Spanish words are pronounced.

Tonic accent (stress)

Spanish words that end with a vowel, in "n" or "s" and do not have a written accent mark, are stressed on the next-to-last syllable: España, todo, ponen, triste.

Words that end in a consonant different than "n" or "s" and that do not have an accent mark (tilde) are stressed at the end: calor, pincel, moral.

All of the words that are not in one of these groups have an accent mark: papá, nación, sábana, árbol.

Grammar Elements

Articulos

Definite = the	Indefinite = a, an
el	un
la	una
los,las	unos, unas

For euphony, el and un are put before nouns that begin with an accented a: el agua , un águila.

Nouns

Gender: generally nouns ending in o are masculine and those ending in a, -tad, -dad, -tud, -ción, and -sión are femenine

Formation of the femenine: The last vowel is exhanged for an a or an a is added to the last consonant: hermano, hermana; monitor, monitora.

Formation of the plural: Nouns that end in a vowel take a -s in the plural: puerta-puertas. Those that end in a consonant take -es in the plural: flor-flores

Special cases: Nouns that end in -s in the singlur remain the same if the stressed syllable is one other than the last, but -es is added if the last syllable is stressed : el/los paraguas; país, países.

Nouns ending in -z form the plural with -ces: la vez-las veces

Qualifying Adjectives

Qualifying adjectives agree in gender and number with their corresponding nouns. Adjectives that end in -o form the femenine by exchanging the o for an a: bonito-bonita. Those that end in e or a consonant have the same ending in masculine and femenine: verde, kibre, feliz, cortés.
Those that indicate nationality add -a in the femenine:
español-española; alemán-alemana.
Plural: is formed the same as with nouns

Comparatives

Of equality: tan...como
Of superiority: más...que
Of inferiority: menos...que

Some common irregular ones are: mayor, menor, mejor, and peor.

Superlative
Relative: el/la/los/las/ más...

Absolute: 1. muy...
2. Adding a suffix to the adjective

Pronouns
Personal pronouns

I	me
you	you
he	him
she	her
you	you
we	us
you (pl.)	you (pl.)
them	them
you (pl.)	you (pl.)

In order to direct what you are saying to a person with whom you do not use the familiar tú form you should use the pronoun usted (abbreviated ud.). The verb that follows is put in 3rd person singular. To direct what say to various people, use ustedes (abbreviated Uds.). The verb is put in 3rd person plural

Grammar

As the complement of a preposition, the forms
yo and tú change into mí, ti: para mí, a ti.
After the preposition con the forms conmigo
and contigo are used

Often the personal pronoun is omitted .
Subject: te qiuero.....

Reflexive pronouns

myself, yourself, him,herself, ourselves,
youselves, theirselves

Adjectives

my
your
his/her, their
our
your (plural)

Pronouns

mine
yours
his, hers
ours
yours theirs

Dimonstrative Adjectives and Pronouns

Adjectives

this, that, that (masculine)
this, that, that (femenine)
these, those, those (plural)

Pronouns

close to the speaker:

this one (m.), this one (f.)
these (m.), these (f.)

Near the speaker

that one (m.), that one (f.)
those (m.), those (f.)

Furthest from the speaker

that one (m.), that one (f.)
those (m.), those (f.)

Relative pronouns

who	that
that, what , which	whose
that, which	those,which

Interrogative adjectives and pronouns

who?   which/which ones
what?

Indefinite adjectives and pronouns

Adjectives and pronouns

some	other
each	such
certain	all
same	various
none	

Pronouns

something	the one, the other
someone	nothing
each one	no one
whichever	one

Adverbs

Of time

then	already
after	tomarrow
then	still
before	yesterday

the day before yesterday	never
today	alot of time
right now	late
soon	early, soon
first, before	the day after tomorrow

Of place

around	up there
inside	down there
outside	to the right
behind	to the left
under	far
on top	where
in front	all over
here	near
there	there

Of frequency

always	never
often	sometimes
every once in a while	ever

Of affirmation/negation

yes	of course
no	sure

| truthfully | absolutely not |
| of course | |

Of quantity

enough	less
alot	so much
hardly	very
a little	too much
more	nothing

Interrogatives

how?	why?
where?	when?
how many?	for what?

Manner of action

like that	better
well	little by little
together	quickly
badly	slowly

You can also form an adverb by adding the suffix -mente to the femenine form of the adjective: lentamente.

Prepositions

| to, at | in between |
| in addition | towards |

with	until
against	for
of, from	for
from	according to
during	without
in	about

Conjunctions

and	like, how
or	when
also	while
neither	because
but	if
nonetheless	even though
in order to	therefore
that	well
neither	since, although

Verbs

Spanish verbs are divided in 3 groups

1. -ar

2. -er

3. -ir

Grammar

The personal pronoun of the subject is generally omitted in front of the verb.

Negative form. The adverb of negation does not always preceed the verb. This includes the past and perfect tenses.

Interrogative form. If the subject pronoun is expressed, it goes behing the verb: ¿Ha estado Julián?
If the pronoun is not expressed, the interrogative does not differ from the ordinary conjugation: ¿Quieres tomar una cerveza?

In Spanish, a question is enclosed by two question marks: ¿...?
To form compound tenses, the auxiliar verb "haber" and the participle are always used. -Ar verbs end en -ado; -er and -ir verbs end in -ido: ¿Habéis ido?

Verbos regulares
indicativo

Presente	Pretérito Imperfecto
hablo,	hablaba
hablas,	hablabas
habla,	hablaba
hablamos,	hablábamos
hablais	hablábais
hablan	hablaban

Pretérito Indefinido	*Futuro*
hablé	hablaré
hablaste	hablarás
habló	hablará
hablamos	hablaremos
hablásteis	hablaréis
hablaron	hablarán

Pretérito Pluscuamperfecto

he hablado
has hablado
ha hablado
hemos hablado
habéis hablado
han hablado

Condicional	**Imperativo**	**Subjuntivo**
hablaría	habla	*Presente*
hablarías	hable	hable
hablaría	hablemos	hables
hablaríamos	hablad	hable
hablaríais	hablen	hablemos
hablarían		habléis
		hablen

Grammar

Imperfecto	Presente Imperfecto	Pretérito
hablara		
hablaras	como,	comía
hablara	comes,	comías
habláramos	come,	comía
habláseis	comemos,	comíamos
hablasen	coméis	comíais
	comen	comían

Pretérito Indefinido	Futuro
comí	comeré
comistes	comerás
comió	comerá
comimos	comeremos
comisteis	comeréis
comieron	comerán

Pretérito Pluscuamperfecto

he comido

has comido

ha comido

hemos comidos

habéis comidos

han comido

Condicional	Imperativo	Subjuntivo
comería	come	*Presènte*
comerías	coma	coma
comería	comamos	comas
comeríamos	comed	coma
comeríais	coman	comamos
comerían		comáis
		coman

Imperfecto	*Presente Imperfecto*	*Pretérito*
comiese		
comieses	vivo,	vivía
comiese	vives,	vivías
comiésemos	vive,	vivía
comiéseis	vivimos	vivíamos
comiesen	vivís	vivíais
	viven	vivían

Pretérito Indefinido	*Futuro*
viví	viviré
viviste	vivirás
vivió	vivirá
vivimos	viviremos
vivisteis	viviréis
vivieron	vivirán

Pretérito Pluscuanperfecto
he vivido
has vivido
ha vivido
hemos vivido
habéis vivido
han vivido

Condicional	**Imperativo**	**Subjuntivo**
viviría	vive	*Presente*
vivirías	viva	viva
viviría	vivamos	vivas
viviríamos	vivid	viva
viviríais	vivan	vivamos
vivirían		viváis
		vivan

Imperfecto
viviese
vivieses
viviese
viviésemos
viviéseis
viviesen

Grammar

Verbos irregulares

Verbo ser

Presente	Pretérito indefinido	Imperfecto
soy	fui	era
eres	fuiste	eras
es	fue	era
somos	fuimos	éramos
sois	fuisteis	erais
son	fueron	eran

Verbo haber

Presente	Futuro imperfecto
he	habré
has	habrás
ha	habrá
hemos	habremos
habéis	habréis
han	habrán

Verbo estar

Presente	*Pretérito indefinido*	
estoy	estuve	
estás	estuviste	
está	estuvo	
estamos	estuvimos	
estáis	estuvisteis	
están	estuvieron	

Verbo tener

Presente	*Pretérito Indefinido*	*Futuro Imperfecto*
tengo	tuve	tendré
tienes	tuviste	tendrás
tiene	tuvo	tendrá
tenemos	tuvimos	tendremos
tenéis	tuvisteis	tendréis
tienen	tuvieron	tendrán

Grammar

Verbo hacer

Presente	*Pretérito indefinido*	*Futuro*
hago	hice	haré
haces	hicíste	harás
hace	hizo	hará
hacemos	hicimos	haremos
hacéis	hicísteis	haréis
hacen	hicieron	harán

Verbo decir

Presente	*Pretérito indefinido*	*Futuro imperfecto*
digo	dije	diré
dices	dijiste	dirás
dice	dijo	dirá
decimos	dijimos	diremos
decís	dijísteis	diréis
dicen	dijeron	dirán

Verbo ir	Pretérito	Pretérito
Presente	*indefinido*	*imperfecto*
voy	fui	iba
vas	fuiste	ibas
va	fue	iba
vamos	fuimos	íbamos
vais	fuisteis	íbais
van	fueron	iban

Grammar

1. Commonly used terms, phrases and expressions

1.1. Phrases of etiquette

Good morning, afternoon, evening.	*Buenos días, buenas tardes, noches.*	Bwaynoass deeahss, tahrdayss, noachayss
See you later, tomorrow, soon, in a bit.	*Hasta luego, mañana, pronto, ahora.*	Ahstah lwaygoa Mahñahnah, Proantoa, ahoarah
Hello, goodbye.	*Hola, adiós.*	Oalah, ahdhyoss
Welcome.	*Bienvenido.*	Byanynbhayneedoass
Have a good trip.	*Tenga usted un buen viaje.*	Tayngah oostaydh oon bwayn bhyahkhay
Have you had a good trip?	*¿Ha tenido usted un buen viaje?*	Ah tayneedoa oostaydh oon bwayn bhyahkhay?
Yes, thank you.	*Sí, gracias.*	See, grahthyahss
Let me introduce to you Mr. (mister), Mrs. (mistress)	*Le presento al señor, a la señora...*	Lay praysayntoa ahl sayñor ah lah sayñorah...
It´s nice to meet you.	*Encantado de conocerle.*	aynkahntahdoa day koanoathayrlay.

How are you?	¿Cómo está usted?	Koamoa aystahoostaydh?
What is your name?	¿Cómo se llama?	Koamoa say yahmah?
How old are you?	¿Cuántos años tiene?	Kwahntoass añoass tyaynay?
How old are you?	¿Qué edad tiene?	Kay aydahdh tyaynay?
Very well, thank you, and you?	Muy bien, gracias, ¿y usted?	Mwee byayn grahthyahss, ee oostaydh?
My name is...	Me llamo...	May yahmoa...
Please, thank you, you´re welcome.	Por favor, gracias, no hay de qué	Por fahbhor, grahthyahss, noa igh day kay
You´re very kind.	Es usted muy amable.	Ayss oostaydh mwee ahmahblay
Please don´t concern yourself with...	No se moleste usted en...	Noa say moalaystay oostaydh ayn...
I´m very sorry.	Lo siento mucho.	Loa syayntoa moochoa
It´s no bother, I´m glad to do it.	No es una molestia, con mucho gusto.	Noa ayss oonah moalaystyah, kon moochoa goostoa

I agree with you.	*Estoy de acuerdo con usted.*	*Aystoy day ahkwayrdoa kon oostaydh*
Whenever/however you like.	*Cuando, como usted quiera.*	*Kwahndoa, koamoa oostaydh kyayrah*
I'm very happy, I'm very comfortable here.	*Estoy muy contento, me encuentro bien aquí.*	*Aystoy mwee koantayntoa, may aynkwayntroa byayn ahkee.*
Pardon me, excuse me.	*Usted perdone.*	*Oostaydh payrdhoanay*
I'm sorry to bother you.	*Siento molestarle.*	*Syayntoa moalaystahrlay*
I'm afraid it will not be possible.	*Me temo que no será posible.*	*May taymoa kay noa sayrah poaseeblay*

1.2. General phrases

Why?	*¿Por qué?*	*Por kay?*
How many?	*¿Cuánto?*	*Kwahntoa?*
Yes, no, never, never, I don't know.	*Sí, no, nunca, jamás, no lo sé*	*See, noa, noonkah khahmahss, noa loa say*
Impossible.	*Imposible.*	*Poaseeblay*

Possible.	*Posible.*	*Poaseeblay*
A lot, nothing, a little.	*Mucho, nada, poco.*	*Moochoa, nahdh poakoa*
Do you speak English, French, Italian, German, Spanish?	*¿Habla usted inglés, francés, italiano, alemán, español?*	*Ahblah oostaydh eenglayss, frahnthayss, eetahlyahnoa, ahlaymahn ayspahñoal*
Can you tell me...?	*¿Puede decirme...?*	*Pwaydhay daytheermay....?*
Can you give me...?	*¿Puede darme...?*	*Pwaydhay dahrmay...?*
What would you like?	*¿Qué desea usted?*	*Kay daysayah oostaydh?*
Can you help me, please?	*¿Puede ayudarme, por favor?*	*Pwaydhay ahyoodahrmay por fahbhor?*
What can I do for you?	*¿En qué puedo servirle?*	*Ayn kay pwaydhoa sayrveerlay?*
What does this mean, that?	*¿Qué significa esto, aquello?*	*Kay seegneefeekah aystoa, ahkayyoa?*
Are you sure?	*¿Está usted seguro?*	*Aystah oostaydh saygooroa.*
I´m sure, very sure.	*Seguro, muy seguro.*	*Saygooroa, mwee saygooroa.*

Thank you for the information.	*Gracias por la información.*	*Grahthyahss por lah eenformahthyon*
Call me on the telephone.	*Llámeme por teléfono.*	*Yahmahmay por taylayfoanoa*
It doesn't matter.	*No tiene importancia.*	*Noa tyaynay eemportahnthyah*
It's important.	*Es importante.*	*Ayss eemportahntay*
Do you understand me well?	*¿Me comprende usted bien?*	*May koampraynday oostaydh byayn*
Yes, I understand you.	*Sí le comprendo.*	*See lay koamprayndoa*
I don't understand you, please speak more slowly.	*No le comprendo, hábleme un poco más despacio, por favor.*	*Noa lay koamprqyndoa, ahblaymay oon poakoa mahss dayspahthyoa por fahbhor*
I'm lost, how can I get out of here, get to...?	*Me he perdido, ¿cómo puedo salir de aquí, llegar a...?*	*May ay payrdheedhoa, koamoa pwaydhoa sahleer day ahkee, yaygahr ah...?*
Listen to me! Hear me out!	*¡Escúcheme! ¡Óigame!*	*Ayskoochaymay Oigahmay*
I'm listening.	*Escucho.*	*Ayskoochoa*

Please wait a moment.	*Espere un momento, por favor.*	*Ayspayray oon moamayntoa por fahbhor*
In a hurry.	*De prisa.*	*Day preesah*
Urgent.	*Urgente.*	*Oorkhayntay*
Help!	*¡Socorro!*	*Soakorroa*
Help!	*¡Ayuda!*	*Ahyoodah*
Call a...	*Llamen a un, una...*	*Lyahmayn ah oon, oonah...*
I would like to make a formal complaint against, for	*Deseo formular una denuncia contra, por...*	*Daysayoa formoolar oonah daynoonthyah kontrah, por....*
I have been robbed.	*Me han robado.*	*May ahn roabahdoa*
I have to call .... urgently.	*Tengo que llamar urgentemente a...*	*Tayngoa kay yahmahr oorkhayntaymanta y ah...*
Follow me!	*¡Sígame!*	*Seegahmay*
I would like, we would like.	*Querría, querríamos.*	*Kayhrreeah, kayhrreeahmoass*
Horrible.	*Horrible.*	*Orreeblay*

What a pity!	¡Qué lástima!	Kay lahsteemah
How ugly!	¡Qué feo!	Kay fayoa
How pretty!	¡Qué bonito!	kayboaneetoa
Unfortunately.	Desgraciada-mente.	Dayssgrahthyahda hmayntay
Fortunately.	Afortunada-mente.	Ahfortoonahdahma yntay
How interesting!	¡Qué interesante!	Kay eentayraysahntay
How lucky!	¡Qué suerte!	Kay swayrtay
What bad luck!	¡Qué mala suerte!	Kay mahlah swayrtay

1.3. Signs and posters

For rent.	Se alquila.	Say ahlkeelah
Stop.	Alto.	Ahltoa
Beware.	Atención.	Ahtaynthyon
Danger.	Peligro.	Payleegroa
Beware of dog.	Cuidado con el perro.	Kweedahdoa kon ayl payrroa
Go ahead.	Pasen.	Pahsyan

Tourist office.	*Oficina de turismo.*	*Oafeetheenah day tooreesmoa*
Customs.	*Aduana.*	*Ahdwahnah*
Airport.	*Aeropuerto.*	*Ahehroapwayrtoa*
Train station.	*Estación de ferrocarril.*	*Aystahthyon day fehrrokahrreel*
Bus stop.	*Parada de autobús.*	*Pahrahdah day owtoabhooss*
Taxi stop.	*Parada de taxis.*	*Pahrahdah day tahkseess*
Do not...	*Prohibido...*	*Proaeebeedhoa*
Closed for vacation, reparations, rest.	*Cerrado por vacaciones, obras, descanso.*	*Thayrradoa por bhahkahthyonays oabrahs, dayskahnsoa*
Close the door.	*Cierren la puerta.*	*Thyayrrayn lah pwayrtah*
No vacancy.	*Completo.*	*koamplaytoa*
Luggage lockers.	*Consigna de equipajes.*	*Koanseegnah day aykeepahkhayss*
Toilets, restrooms, women, men.	*Lavabos, señoras, caballeros.*	*Lahbhahbosa, sayñorahs, kahbahyayroass*

Information.	*Información.*	*Eenformahthyon*
Reception.	*Recepción.*	*Raythaypthyon*
Detour.	*Desviación.*	*Daysbhyahthyon*
No passing, bathing, hunting, fishing.	*Prohibido pasar, bañarse, cazar, pescar.*	*Proaeebeedoa pahsahr, bahñahrsay cahthar, payskahr*
Do not litter.	*Prohibido arrojar basuras.*	*Proaeebeedoa ahrroakhahr bahsoorahss*
No smoking.	*Prohibido fumar.*	*Proaeebeedoa foomahr*
Do not feed the animals.	*Prohibido dar de comer a los animales.*	*Proeebeedoa dahr day losmayr ah loass ahneemahlayss*
No camping.	*Prohibido acampar.*	*Proaeebeedoa ahkahmpahr*
No minors allowed.	*Prohibida la entrada a menores.*	*Proaeebeedah lah ayntrahdah ah maynorayss*
Smoking area.	*Zona de fumadores.*	*Thoanah day foomahdhorayss*
Parking.	*Estacionamiento*	*Aystahthyonahmyayntoa*
Parking.	*Aparcamiento*	*Ahpahrkahmyayntoa*
Entrance.	*Entrada.*	*Ayntrahdah*

Exit.	*Salida.*	*Sahleedhah*
Emergency exit.	*Salida de emergencia.*	*Sahleedhah day aymayrkhanyn-thyah*
Arrivals.	*Llegada.*	*Yaygahdhah*
Sold out.	*Agotado.*	*Ahgoatahdhoa*
Out of service.	*No funciona.*	*Noa foonthyoanah*
Free admission.	*Entrada libre.*	*Ayntrahdah leebray*
For sale.	*Se vende.*	*Say baynday*
Do not speak to the driver.	*No hablen al conductor.*	*Noa ahblayn ahl knodooktor*
Do not disturb.	*No molestar.*	*Noa moalaystahr*
Do not touch.	*No tocar.*	*Noa toakahr*
Busy.	*Ocupado.*	*Oakoopahdoa*
Toll.	*Peaje.*	*Payahkhay*
Crosswalk.	*Paso de peatones.*	*Pahsoa day payahtoanays*
Private property.	*Propiedad privada.*	*Propyaydhadh preebhahdhah*
Residents only.	*Sólo para residentes.*	*Soaloa pahrah rayseedayntayss*

Waiting room.	*Sala de espera.*	*Sahlah day ayspayrah*
Sale.	*Rebajas.*	*Raybahkhahss*
Dressing room.	*Vestuarios.*	*Bhaystooahryoass*
Ring the bell.	*Llamar al timbre.*	*Yahmahr ahl teembray*

1.4. Family and friends

Have you met my friends?	*¿Conoces a mis amigos?*	*koanoathayss ah meess ahmeegoass?*
Have you met my girlfriend?	*¿Conoces a mi novia?*	*Koanoathayss ah mee noabhyah?*
Let me introduce you to my brothers and their children.	*Te presento a mis hermanos y a sus hijos.*	*Tay praysayntoa ah meess ayrmahnoass ee ah sooss eekhoass*
How is your wife?	*¿Cómo está tu mujer?*	*Koamoa aystah too mookhayr*
Are you married?	*¿Está usted casado?*	*Aystah oostaydh kahsahdhoa?*
No, I'm single.	*No, soy soltero.*	*Noa, soi soltayroa*
My father, my mother and my grandparents live with me.	*Mi padre, mi madre y mis abuelos viven conmigo.*	*Mee pahdray, mee mahdray, ee meess ahbwayloass bheebhayn konmeegoa.*

How many children do you have?	¿Cuántos hijos tiene usted?	Kwahntoass eekhoass tyaynay oostaydh?
I have two sons and one daughter, my daughter is the youngest.	Tengo dos niños y una niña, mi hija es la menor.	Tayngoa doss neeñoass ee oonah neeñah, mee eekhah ayss lah maynor
Have you come only to...?	¿Ha venido sólo a...?	Ah bhayneedhoa soaloa ah...?
No, I have come to see some relatives, with my son.	No, he venido a ver a unos parientes, con mi hijo.	Noa ay bhayneedhoa ah bhayr ah oonoass pahryayntays kon mee eekhoa
Has it been long since you married?	¿Hace mucho que están ustedes casados?	Ahthay moochoa kay aystahn oostaydhayss kahsahdoass?
Do you want to get a drink, to go see a movie, tonight?	¿Vienes a tomar una copa, al cine, esta noche?	Bhyaynays ah toamahr oonah coapah ahl theenay aystah noachay?
Can I bring a friend, my cousin, my sister?	¿Puedo llevar a un amigo, a mi prima, mi hermana?	Pwaydhoa yaybhar ah oon ahmeegoa, ah mee preemah, mee ayrmahnah?
I would love to, but tonight	Me encantaría, pero esta	May aynkahntahreeah

I want to rest from my trip, how about tomorrow?	*noche quiero descansar del viaje, ¿por qué no mañana?*	*payroa aystah dayscahnsahr dayl bhyahkhay, por kay noa mahñahnah?*
Would you like to have dinner with me?	*¿Puedo invitarte a cenar?*	*Pwaydhoa eenveetahrtay ah thaynahr?*
Do you mind if I sit here?	*¿Le importa si me siento aquí?*	*Lay eemportah see may syayntoa ahkeeh?*
Are you waiting for someone?	*¿Está usted esperando a alguien?*	*Aystah oostaydh ayspayrahndoa ah ahlgyayn?*
May I go with you to your hotel?	*¿Puedo acompañarle hasta su hotel?*	*Pwaydhoa ahkompahñahrla ah ahlgyayn?*
I would like to see you tomorrow.	*Me gustaría verla mañana.*	*May goostahreeah bhayrlah mahñahnah*
I'll pick you up at the hotel.	*Iré a recogerte al hotel.*	*Eeray ah raykoakhayrtay ahl oatayl.*
Where can we meet?	*¿Dónde podemos quedar?*	*Doandhay poadhaymoass kaydhahr?*

Vocabulary

English	Spanish	Pronunciation
grandmother	*abuela*	*ahbwehlah*
grandfather	*abuelo*	*ahbwehloa*
friend	*amigo*	*ahmeegoa*
friendship	*amistad*	*ahmeestahdh*
love	*amor*	*ahmor*
kiss	*beso*	*baysoa*
affection	*cariño*	*kahreeñoa*
to get married	*casarse*	*kahsahrsah*
date, appointment	*cita*	*theetah*
acquaintance	*conocido*	*koanoatheedoa*
brother-in-law	*cuñado*	*kooñahdoa*
divorced	*divorciado*	*deebhortheeahdoa*
family	*familia*	*fahmeelyah*
sister	*hermana*	*ayrmahnah*
brother	*hermano*	*ayrmahnoa*
older	*mayor*	*mahyor*
younger	*menor*	*maynor*
daughter	*hija*	*eekhah*
son	*hijo*	*eekhoa*
invitation	*invitación*	*eenbheetahthyon*
mother	*madre*	*mahdray*
husband	*marido*	*mahneedoa*
wife	*mujer*	*mookhayr*
grandson	*nieto*	*nyayto*

child	*niño*	*neeñoa*
girlfriend	*novia*	*noabyah*
daughter-in-law	*nuera*	*nwehrah*
father	*padre*	*pahdray*
relative	*pariente*	*pahryayntay*
cousin	*primo*	*preemoa*
relationship	*relación*	*raylahthyon*
Mr. (mister)	*señor*	*sayñor*
Mrs. (mistress)	*señora*	*saynorah*
Miss	*señorita*	*saynoreetah*
nice	*simpático*	*seempahteekoa*
nephew	*sobrino*	*soabreenoa*
mother-in-law	*suegra*	*swehgrah*
father-in-law	*suegro*	*swehgroa*
uncle	*tío*	*teeoa*
aunt	*tía*	*teeah*
widow	*viuda*	*byoodah*
widower	*viudo*	*byoodoa*
son-in-law	*yerno*	*yayrhoa*

2. Travel

2.1. Travel arrangements

I would like to make a reservation for two plane tickes for...	*Deseo reservar dos billetes de avión para...*	*Daysayoa rayssayrvahr doss beeyaytayss day ahbhyon pahrah...*
Do you have pre-arranged trips for one, two, three weeks for...?	*¿Tienen ustedes viajes organizados de una, dos, tres semanas para...?*	*Tyayanyn oostaydhayss bhyahkhays orgahneethahdhoas day oona, doss, trayss saymahnahss pahrah...?*
How much is the price of the fare per person?	*¿Cuál es el precio del viaje por persona?*	*Kwahl ays ayl praythyoa dayl bhyakhay por payrsoanah?*
What form of payment can I use?	*¿Qué forma de pago me ofrecen?*	*Kay formah day pahgoa may oafraythayn*
I would like for you to make a reservation in hotels of three, four, stars.	*Deseo que me reserven el alojamiento en hoteles de tres, cuatro, estrellas.*	*Daysayoa kay may raysayrbhayn ayl ahloakhahmyehntoa ayn oataylayss day trayss, kwahtroa, aystrayahss*
I would like to rent an apartment ocean side.	*Deseo alquilar un apartamento en primera línea de playa.*	*Daysayoa ahlkeelahr oon ahpahrtahmayntoa ayn preemayrah leenayah day plahyah.*
I would like to confirm,	*Quiero confirmar,*	*Kyayroa konfeermahr,*

cancel my flight reservation, my ticket...	*cancelar mi reserva para el viaje, billete...*	*kahnthaylahr mee raysayrbya pyarya ayl beeyakhay, beeyaytya...*
Do you have any pamphlets, maps, guides...?	*¿Tiene folletos, mapas, planos...?*	*Teeaynay foayhaitoadd, myapyas, plyanoas...*

2.2. Customs

Passport control.	*Control de pasaportes.*	*Kontoal day pahsahportays*
Your passport, please.	*Su pasaporte, por favor.*	*Soo pahsahportay por fahbhor*
Do you have anything to declare?	*¿Tiene usted algo que declarar?*	*Tyaynay oostaydh ahlgoa kay dayklahrahr?*
No, I don't have anything to declare.	*No tengo nada que declarar.*	*Noa tayngoa nahdah kay dayklahrahr*
I have a bottle of liquor and a carton of cigarrettes.	*Tengo una botella de licor y un cartón de cigarrillos.*	*Tayngoa oonah boatayyah day leekohr ee oon kahrtoan day theegahrreeyoass*
Open this suitcase, please.	*Abra esta maleta, por favor.*	*Ahbrah aystah mahlaytah por fahbhoar*
May I close the suitcase, bag, briefcase?	*¿Puedo cerrar ya la maleta, la bolsa, el maletín?*	*Pwaydhoa thayrrahr yah lah mahlaytah, lah boalsah, ayl mahlayteen?*

These things are for personal use.	*Estos son objetos para mi uso personal.*	*Aystoadd soan oabkhaytoadd pahrah mee oosoa payrsoanahl*
You'll have to pay taxes for this.	*Tendrá que pagar impuestos por esto.*	*Tayndrah kay pahgahr eempwenstoass por aystoa*
Where is the money exchange office?	*¿Dónde está la oficina de cambios?*	*Doanday austah lah oafeetheenah day kambyoass?*
My wife and children are with me.	*Me acompañan mi mujer y mis hijos, hijas.*	*May ahkoampahñahn mee mookhayr ee meess eekhoass, eekhahss.*
My personal information is...	*Mis datos personales son...*	*Meess dahtoass payrsoanahlayss soan...*
I will be here for fifteen days.	*Estaré quince días.*	*Aystahray keenthay deehass*
Please, the entry visa, the stay visa, de exit visa.	*Por favor, el visado de entrada, estancia, salida.*	*Por fahbhor, ayl bheesahdhoa day ayntrahdhah aystahnthyah, sahleedhah*
Personal docummentation, car docummentation.	*Documentación personal, del vehículo.*	*Doakoomayntahthy on payrsoanahl, dayl bhayeekooloa*

Vocabulary

duty	*aranceles*	*ahrahnthaylayss*
taxes	*impuestos*	*eempwehstoass*
tourist office	*oficina de turismo*	*oafeetheenah day tooreesmoa*
cancelation	*cancelación*	*kanthaylahthyon*
confirmation	*confirmación*	*konfeermahthyon*
vacations, holidays	*vacaciones*	*bhahkahthyonays*
itenarary	*itinerario*	*eeteenayrahryoa*
visas	*visados*	*bheeshdhoass*
vaccines	*vacunaciones*	*bhahkoonahthonays*
travel insurance	*seguro de viaje*	*saygooroa day bhyahkhay*
translator	*intérprete*	*eentayrpraytay*
driver´s license	*permiso de conducir*	*payrmeesoa day kondootheer*
police	*policía*	*poaleetheeah*
name and last name, surname	*nombre y apellidos*	*noambray ee ahpayeedoass*
nationality	*nacionalidad*	*nahthyonahleedhadh*
luggage, baggage	*equipaje*	*aykeepahkhay*
duty	*derechos de aduana*	*dayraychoass day ahdwahnah*

2.3. Money

2.3.1. Bancos, cambios de moneda

Could you please tell me where is there a bank?	*¿Por favor, me puede indicar dónde hay una sucursal bancaria?*	*Por fahbhor, may pwaydhay eendeekahr doanday igh oonah sookoorsahl bahnkahryah?*

Where can I change money?	¿Dónde puedo cambiar moneda?	Doanday pwaydhoa kahmbyahr moanaydhah?
Where is there a cash machine?	¿Dónde hay un cajero automático?	Doanday ish oon kakhayroa owtoamahteekoa?
Could you change these dollars for local currency?	¿Puede cambiarme estos dólares en moneda del país?	Pwaydhay kahmbyahrmay aystoass doalahrayss ayn moanaydhah dayl paheess?
What is the exchange rate today?	¿A cuánto está el cambio hoy?	Ah kwahntoa aystah ayl kahmbyoa oi?
What is the exchange rate for the peseta, the mark, the pound?	¿Cuál es el cambio de la peseta, el marco, la libra?	Kwahl ayss ayl kahmbyoa day lah paysaytah, ayl mahrkoa, lah leebrah?
Could you give me large bills, small bills, coins?	¿Podría darme billetes grandes, pequeños, monedas?	Poadreeah dharmay beeyaytayss grahndays, paykaynoas, moanaydhahss?
I would like to know if I have received a transfer to my account for ..?	¿Querría saber si he recibido una transferencia a mi cuenta por importe de...?	Kehrreeah sahbayr see ay raytheebeedoa oonah trahnsfayraynthyah ah mee kwayntah por eemportay day...?
Your balance is at zero.	No tiene saldo.	Noa tyaynay sahldoa

I would like to open an account in this bank.	*Quisiera abrir una cuenta en este banco.*	*Keessyayrah ahbreer oonah kwayntah ayn aystay bahnkoa*
I would like to close my account.	*Deseo cancelar mi cuenta.*	*Daysayoa kahnthaylahr mee kwayntah*
Could I cash this check?	*¿Es posible cobrar este cheque?*	*Ayss poaseeblay koabrahr aystay chaykay?*
You have a negative balance.	*Está usted con saldo deudor.*	*Aystah oostaydh kon sahldoa dayoohdhor.*
Could you tell me how much cash is available in my account?	*¿Puede indicarme el saldo disponible de mi cuenta?*	*Pwaydhay eendeekahrmay ayl sahldoa deespoaneeblay daydaykhahr soo*
I would like to make a transfer, a deposit to account number... for...	*Deseo hacer una transferencia, un ingreso a la cuenta número... de...*	*Daysayoa eengrayshar oonah trahsfayraynthyah, oon eengraysoa ah lah kwayntah noomayroa... day...*
I would like to deposit this check in my account.	*Deseo ingresar este cheque en mi cuenta.*	*Daysayoa eengraysahr aystay chaykay ayn mee kwayntah*
Could I change these traveller´s checks?	*¿Puedo cambiar estos cheques de viaje?*	*Pwaydhoa kahmbyahr aystoas chaykayss day byahkhay?*

Could you leave me your identification document, your passport?	¿Me puede dejar su carnet de identidad, pasaporte?	May pwaydhay mee kwayntah? kahrnayt day eedaynteedhadh, passahportay?
I have lost my credit card.	He perdido mi tarjeta de crédito.	Ay payrdheedhoa mee thrkhaytah day kraydheetoa
Please, go to the teller.	Pase por caja, por favor.	Pahsay por kahkhah, por fahbhor.
Please, sign here.	Firme aquí, por favor.	Feermay ahkee, por fahbhor.

Vocabulary

stocks	acciones	ahktheeoanayss
savings	ahorro	ahohrroa
bank	banco	bahnkoa
bill	billete	beeyaytay
security deposit box	caja de seguridad	kahkhah day saygooreedhadh
teller	cajero	kakhayroa
cash	cobro en efectivo	koabroa ayn ayfaykteebhoa
credit	crédito	kraydheetoa
deposit	depósito	daypoaseetoa
discount.	descuento	dayskwayntoa
debtor	deudor	dayoohdhor
currency	divisa	deebheesah
document.	documento	doakoomayntoa
receipt, invoice	factura	fahktoorah
out of circulation	fuera de circulación	fwehrah day theerkoolahthyon

expenditures, expenses	gastos	gahstoas
tour guide	guía turístico	geeah tooreesteekah
mortgage	hipoteca	eepoataykah
imprint	impreso	eempraysoa
interest	interés	eentayrays
investment	inversión	eenbhayrsyon
bill of exchange, draft	letra de cambio	laytrah day kahmbyoa
currency.	moneda	moanaydhah
national bills	moneda nacional	moanaydhah nahthyonahl
cash payment	pago en efectivo	pahgoa ayn ayfaykteebhoa
percentage	porcentaje	porsayntahkhay
loan	préstamo	praystaymoa
refund	reembolso	rayehmboalsoa
check book	talonario de cheques	tahloanahryoa day chaykays
transfer	transferencia	trahnsfayraynthyah
overdue	vencimiento	bhayntheemyayntoa
window	ventanilla	bhayntahneelyah

2.4. Automobiles

2.4.1. Car rental

I would like to rent a car with a driver, without a driver.	Desearía alquilar un coche con chófer, sin chófer.	Daysayahreea ahlkeelahr oon koachay kon choafayr, seen choafayr

What cars do you have available?	¿Qué coches tienen disponibles?	Kay koachayss tyaynayn deespoaneeblayss?
How much is the car rental per day and per kilometre?	¿Cuánto cuesta el alquiler por día y por kilómetro?	Kwahntoa kwaystah ayl ahlkeelayr por deeah ee por keeloamaytroa?
And for a weekend?	¿Y para un fin de semana?	Ee pahrah oon feen day saymahnah?
Is the insurance included?	¿Está incluido el seguro?	Austah eenklooeedoan ayl saygooroa?
When can I pick it up?	¿Cuándo lo puedo recoger?	Kwahndhoa loapwaydho9a raykoakhayr?
Do I need to leave a deposit?	¿Es necesario algún tipo de fianza?	Ayss naythaysahryoa ahlgoon teepo day feeahnthah?
Is the documentation in the car?	¿Está en el coche la documentación?	Aystah ayn ayl koachay lah doakoomayntahthyon?
Do you have a branch in the city..., could I leave the car there when I get there?	¿Tienen ustedes sucursal en la ciudad..., puedo dejar allí el coche cuando llegue?	Tyaynayn oostaydhayss sookoorsahl ayn lah thyoodhadh..., pwaydhoa daykhahr ahyee ayl koachay kwahndoa yaygay?

2.4.2. Roads and Highways

Could you tell me where is the highway, the main road of the city...?	¿Puede indicarme la dirección hacia la autopista, carretera de la ciudad...?	*Pwayday eendeekahrmay lah deeraykthyon ahthyah lah owtoapeestah, kahrraytayrah day lah thyoodhadh?*
How many kilometres away is...?	¿Cuántos kilómetros hay hasta...?	*Kwahntoass keeloamaytroass igh ahstah...?*
Is this the road to the station, airport...?	¿Es ésta la carretera para ir a la estación, el aeropuerto...?	*Ayss aystah lah kahrraytayrah pahrah eer ah lah aystahthyon, ayl ahehroapwayrtoa...?*
You are on the wrong road.	Se ha equivocado de carretera.	*Say ah aykeebhoakahdhoa day kahrraytayrah.*
Go back where you came from, you are going the opposite way.	Vuelva atrás, va usted en dirección contraria.	*Bhwaylbhah ahtrahss, bhah oostaydh ayn deerraykthyon kontrahryah.*
Go straight ahead until you reach the square	Siga todo recto hasta la plaza.	*Seegah todhoa rayktoa ahstah lah plahthah.*
Turn to the left, the right.	Doble a la izquierda, derecha.	*Doablay ah lah eethkyayrdhah, dayraychah.*
Is it a good road?	¿Es buena la carretera?	*Ayss bwaynah lah kahrraytayrah?*

Is it dangerous?	¿Es peligrosa?	Ayss payleegroasah?
Go to the first intersection.	Vaya hasta el primer cruce.	Bhahyah ahstah aylpreemayr kroothay.
Could you show me on this map where we are.	¿Puede señalar en este mapa dónde me encuentro?	Pwaydhay sayñahlahr ayn aystah mahpah doandhay may aynkwayntroa?
Which is the best road, the shortest, the most interesting, the quickest to go to...?	¿Cuál es el mejor camino, el más corto, el más interesante, el más rápido para ir a...?	Kwahl ayss ayl maykhor kahmeenoa, ayl mahss kortoa, ayl mahss eentayraysahntay, ayl mahss rahpeedoa pahrah eer ah...?
Could you give me a roadmap? Where can I get one?	¿Me puede facilitar un mapa de carreteras? ¿Dónde puedo conseguirlo?	May pwaydhay fahtheeleetahr oon mahpah day kahrraytayrahss? Doanday pwaydhoa konsaygeerloa?
Is there a city nearby? a hotel? a place where I can spend the night?	¿Hay alguna ciudad cercana? ¿Algún hotel? ¿Algún sitio donde pasar la noche?	Igh ahlgoonah thyoodhad thayrkahnah? Ahlgoon oatayl? Ahlgoon seetyoa doanday pahsahr lah noachay?
Where is the nearest gas station?	¿A qué distancia está la gasolinera más próxima?	Ah kay deestahnthyah aystah lah gahssoaleenayrah mahss proakseemah?
Can I reach downtown in a car?	¿Puedo ir en coche hasta el centro de la ciudad?	Pwaydhoa eer ayn koachay ahstah aylthayntroa day lah thyoodhahdh?

2.4.3. Traffic violations

Let me see your proof of insurance and your driver´s license.	*Déme los papeles del coche y el permiso de conducir.*	*Daymay loass pahpaylayss dayl koachay ee ayl payrmeesoa day kondootheer*
Here is my documentation.	*Aquí tiene los documentos.*	*Ahkee tyaynay loass dhoakoomayntoass.*
I have to give you a ticket, make a report.	*Tengo que ponerle una multa, denunciarle.*	*Tayngoa kay poanayrlay oonah mooltah, daynoonthyahrlay.*
I would like to know the reason.	*Quisiera saber el motivo.*	*Keesyayrah sahbayr ayl moateebhoa.*
You were driving over the speed limit.	*Iba circulando a gran velocidad.*	*Eebah theerkoalahnddhoa ah grahn bhayloatheedhadh.*
You have overlooked a traffic signal.	*Se ha saltado una señal de tráfico.*	*Say ah sahltahdhoa oonah sayñahl day trahfeekoa.*
You didn´t stop in front of the stop sign.	*No ha hecho la parada obligatoria del stop.*	*Noa ah aychoa lah pahrahdhah oableegahtoryah dayl stoap.*
Would you open the trunk of the car?	*¿Puede abrir el maletero del coche?*	*Pwaydhay ahbreer ayl mahlaytayroa dayl koachay?*

I didn't realize I was going so fast.	No me he dado cuenta de que iba a mucha velocidad.	Noa may ay dahdhoa kwayntah day kay eebah ah moochah bhayloatheedhadh.
I didn't see the sign.	No he visto bien la señalización.	Noa ay bheestoa byayn lah sayñahleethahthyon.
How much is the fine?	¿A cuánto asciende la multa?	Ah kwahntoa ahssthyaynday lah mooltah?
Please, sign here.	Firme aquí, por favor.	Feermay ahkee por fahbhor.
Get out of the car!	¡Bájese del coche!	Bahkhaysay dayl koachay!
Stay inside the car!	¡Permanezca dentro del coche!	Payrmyanaythkya dayntro dayl koachay!
Drive carefully.	Circule con precaución.	Theerkoolay kon praykahwthyon.

2.4.4. Service station

| Where is there a gas station? | ¿Dónde hay una estación de servicio? | Doanday ay oonah aystahthyon day sayrbheethyoa? |
| How far is the next gas station? | ¿A qué distancia está la próxima gasolinera? | Ah kaydeestahnthyah aystah lah proakseemah gahssoaleenayrah? |

How much per litre of gas?	¿A qué precio está el litro de gasolina?	*Ah kay praythyoa aystah ayl leetroa day gahssoaleenah?*
I would like to fill up, fill up the tank, please.	Deseo repostar, llene el depósito, por favor.	*Daysayoa raypoastahr, yaynay ayl daypoaseetoa, por fahbhor.*
I would like ... litres of gas.	Quisiera... litros de gasolina.	*keesyayrah... Leetroass day gahssoaleenah.*
I would like a can of oil.	Déme una lata de aceite.	*Daymay oonah lahtah day ahthaytay.*
Check the oil level	Compruebe el nivel del aceite.	*Komprooaybay ayl neebhayl dayl ahthaytay.*
Could you check the air pressure in the tires?	¿Podría comprobar la presión del aire de los neumáticos, las ruedas?	*Podreeah komproabahr lah praysyon dayl ahyray day loass nayoomahteekoass, lahss rwaydahss?*
Could you check the breaks?	¿Podría revisar los frenos?	*Podreeah raybheesahr loass fraynoass?*
Could you please fill the radiator with water?	Por favor, ¿podría ponerme agua en el radiador?	*Por fahbhor, podreeah poanayrmay ahgwah radyadoar*
The windshield wiper does not work.	El limpiaparabrisas no funciona.	*Ayl leempyahpahrahbre esahss noa foonthyonah.*

| I would like to wash the car. | *Quisiera lavar el coche.* | *Keesyayrah ayl koachay.* |
| No thank you, it´s not necessary. | *No, no hace falta, gracias.* | *Noa, noa ahthay fahltah, grahthyahss.* |

2.4.5. Service station (repairs)

How can I call a tow truck to take the car to the repair shop?	*¿Cómo podría llamar a una grúa para que lleve el coche al taller?*	*Koamoa podreeah yahmahr ah oonah grooah pahrah kay yaybhay ayl koachay ayl tahyayr?*
Where is there a repair shop?	*¿Dónde hay un taller de reparaciones?*	*Doanday igh oon tahyayr day raypahrahthyonayss?*
Could you tow my car, please?	*¿Por favor, puede remolcarme?*	*Por fahbhor, pwaydhay raymoalkahrmay?*
How far is the nearest repair shop?	*¿A qué distancia está el taller más próximo?*	*Ah kay deestahnthyah aystah ayl tahyayr mahss proakseemoa?*
The battery is dead.	*La batería está descargada.*	*Lah bahtayreeah aystah daysskahrgahdhah.*
There's something wrong with the engine. It´s making a strange sound.	*Hay una avería en el motor. Se oye un ruido extraño.*	*Igh oonah ahbhayreeah ayn ayl moator. Say oayay oon aykstrahñoa.*
Could you give me an estimate?	*¿Puede darme un presupuesto?*	*Pwaydhay dahrmay oon praysoopwaystoa?*

Is there in this city a Renault repair shop?	¿Hay, en esta ciudad, algún taller de servicio oficial Renault?	Igh, ayn aystah thyoodhahdh, ahlgoon tahyayr day sayrbheethyoa oafeethyahl Raynowlt?
How long will it take to fix it?	¿Cuánto tiempo durará la reparación?	Kwahntoa tyaympoa doorahrah lah raypahrahthyon?
Please, check..., fix...	Por favor, revise..., repare...	Por fahbhor, raybheesay..., raypahray...
Could you change the spark plugs?	¿Puede cambiar las bujías?	Pwayday kahmbyahr lahss bookheeahss?
I have a puncture in my rear left tire.	Tengo un pinchazo en la rueda trasera izquierda.	Tayngoa oon peenchahthoa ayn lah rwaydhah trahsayrah eethkyayrdhah.
The right light bulb is out.	Se fundió la bombilla del faro derecho.	Say foondyoa lah boambeeyah dayl fahroa dayraychoa.

2.4.6 Accidentes

Someone has had an accident at the mile marker..., ... kilometres from here.	Se ha producido un accidente en el kilómetro..., a ... kilómetros de aquí.	Say ah proadootheedhoa oon ahktheedhayntay ayn ayl keebamaytro..., ah ... keeloamaytroass day ahkee.
There is someone badly hurt, slightly hurt.	Hay heridos graves, leves.	Igh ayreedhoass grahbhayss, laybhayss.

Please, call the police.	Por favor, llame a la policía.	Por fahbhor, yahmay ah lah poaleetheeah.
Where is the nearest hospital?	¿Dónde está el hospital más cercano?	Doanday aystah ayl oaspeetahl mahss thayrkahnoa?
Call a doctor!	¡Llamen a un médico!	Yahmayn ah oon maydeekoa!
Call an ambulance right away.	Llamen en seguida a una ambulancia.	Yahmayn ayn saygeedhah ah oonah ahmboolahnthyah.
Are you hurt?	¿Está usted herido?	Aystah oostaydh ayreedhoa?
My insurance company is..., here is my policy.	Mi compañía de seguros es..., aquí está la póliza.	Mee kompahñeeah day saygooroass ayss..., ahkee aystah lah poaleethah.
Please, don´t move!	¡No se mueva!, por favor.	Noa say mwaybhah!, por fahbhor.
Have you been a witness to the accident?	¿Ha sido usted testigo de lo ocurrido?	Ah deedhoa oostaydh taysteegoa day loa oakoorreedhoa?
Could you give me your name and address to find you if I need to?	¿Me puede dar su nombre y dirección para poder localizarle en caso de necesidad?	May pwayday dahr soo noambray ee deeraykthyon pahrah poadhayr loakahleethahrlay ayn kahsoa day naythaydeedhahdh?

| Did you see the number plate of the car that didn't stop? | ¿Ha visto la matrícula del otro vehículo que no ha parado? | *Ah bheestoa lah mahtreekiilah dayl oatroa bhayeekooloakay noa ah pahrahdhoa? yeekooloa kay noa ah pahrahdhoa?* |

Vocabulary

accident	*accidente*	*ahktheedayntay*
accelerator	*acelerador*	*ahthaylayrahdhor*
distilled water	*agua destilada*	*ahgwah daysteelahdhah*
shock	*amortiguador*	*ahmoarteegwahdor*
antifreeze	*anticongelante*	*ahnteekonkhaylahntay*
starter	*arranque*	*ahrrahnkay*
battery	*batería*	*bahtayreeah*
bulb	*bombilla*	*boambeeyah*
spark plug	*bujía*	*bookheeah*
trunk	*capó*	*kahpo*
carburettor	*carburador*	*kahrboorahdor*
frame	*carrocería*	*kahrroathayreeah*
seatbelt	*cinturón de seguridad*	*theentooroan day saygooreedhahdh*
driver	*conductor*	*kondooktor*
crossing	*cruce*	*kroothay*
curve	*curva*	*koorbhah*
chassis	*chasis*	*chahseess*
clutch	*embrague*	*aymbrahgway*
rear-view mirror	*espejo retrovisor*	*ayspaykhoa taytroabheesor*
filter	*filtro*	*feeltroa*
keys	*llaves*	*yahbhayss*

tire	neumático	Naywmahteekoa
spare part	pieza de repuesto	pyaythah day raypwaystoa
radiator	radiador	tahdyahdor
screw	tornillo	torneeyoa
exhaust pipe	tubo de escape	tooboa day ayskahpay

2.5. Trains, the train station

Could you tell me where the train station is?	¿Puede decirme dónde está la estación de ferrocarril?	Pwayday daytheermay doanday aystah lah aystahthyon day fayrrokahrreel?
When does the train leave for?	¿A qué hora sale el tren para...?	Ah kay oarah ahlay ayl trayn pahrah...?
Does the train go directly to...?	¿El tren es directo a...?	Ayl trayn ayss deerayktoa ah...?
What platform does it leave from?	¿Por qué vía, andén sale?	Por kay bheeah, ahndayn sahlay?
Give me a ticket for... first class, second class.	Déme un billete para... de primera, segunda clase.	Daymay oon beeyatay pahrah... day preemayrah, saygoondhah. klahsay.
How much is the ticket to...?	¿Qué cuesta el billete para...?	Kay kwaystah ayl beeyaytay pahrah...?
And a round trip ticket?	¿Y un billete de ida y vuelta?	Ee oon beeyaytay day eedhah ee bwayltah?

Are there coupons for ten, twenty trips?	*¿Tienen bonos de diez, veinte viajes?*	*Tyaynayn boanoas day dyayth, bhayntay bhyahkhayss?*
How long time the train stops here?	*¿Cuánto tiempo para el tren aquí?*	*kwahntoa tyaympoa pahrah ayl trayn ahkee?*
I would like to check in my luggage.	*Quisiera facturar el equipaje.*	*keesyayrah fahktoorahr ayl aykeepahkhay.*

Vocabulary

platform	*andén*	*ahndayn*
ticket	*billete*	*beeyaytay*
bed car	*coche-cama*	*koachay-kahmah*
compartment	*compartimento*	*kompahrteemayntoa*
left luggage-office	*consigna*	*konseegnah*
schedule	*horario*	*oarahryoa*
train station manager	*jefe de estación*	*khayfay day aystahthyon*
bunk	*litera*	*leetarah*
locomotive	*locomotora*	*loakoamoatoarah*
machinist	*maquinista*	*mahkeeneestah*
passenger	*pasajero*	*pahsahkhayroa*
corridor	*pasillo*	*pahseeyoa*
reservation	*reserva*	*raysayrbhah*
ticket reviewer	*revisor*	*raybheesor*
waiting room	*sala de espera*	*sahlah day ayspayrah*
carriage	*vagón*	*bhahgoan*

2.6. Airplane, the airport

How long does it take to get from the hotel to the airport?	¿Cuánto se tarda desde el hotel al aeropuerto?	*Kwahntoa say tahrdhah daysday ayl oatayl ahl ahayroapwayrtoa?*
How early should I be at the airport?	¿Con cuánta antelación debo estar en el aeropuerto?	*Kon kwahntah ahntaylahthyon dayboa aystahr ayn ayl ahayroapwayrtoa?*
I want a first class ticket, an economy ticket, for the flight to...	Quiero un billete de primera clase, de clase turista, para el vuelo a...	*kyayroa oon beeyaytay day preemayrah klahsay, day klahsay tiireestah, pahrah ayl bhwayloa ah...*
I would like to change the date of departure, of return.	Quisiera modificar la fecha de salida, de regreso.	*Keesyayrah modeefeekahrlah faychah day sahleedha, day raygraysoa.*
I would like to confirm my reservation.	Quisiera confirmar el billete.	*Keesyayrah konfeermahr ayl beeyaytay.*
Where is the desk to check in the luggage? the airline company is...	¿Dónde está el mostrador para facturar el equipaje? la compañía aérea es...	*Doanday aystah ayl mostrahdor pahrah fahktiirahr ayl aykeepahkhay? lah kompahñeeah ahayrayah ayss...*
How much is the ticket?	¿Cuánto cuesta el billete?	*kwahntoa kwaystah ayl beeyaytay?*

63

What is maximum luggage weight alowed?	¿Qué límite de peso admiten sin recargo?	Kay leemeetay day paysoa ahdhmeetayn seen raykahrgoa?
What time does the flight leave?	¿A qué hora sale el vuelo?	Ah kay oarah sahlay ayl bhwayloa?
Is there a waiting room?	¿Existe una sala de espera?	Aykseestay oonah sahlah day ayspayrah?
Where is the boarding gate?	¿Cuál es la puerta de embarque?	Kwahl ayss lah pwayrtah day aymbahrkay?
When do we board?	¿A qué hora embarcaremos?	Ah kay oarah aymbahrkahraymoass?
I Would like smoking or non smoking seat.	Quisiera un asiento de fumador, no fumador.	Keeyayrah oon ahsyayntoa day foomahdhor, noa foomahdhor.
I only have carry on luggage.	Sólo llevo equipaje de mano.	Soaloa yaybhoa aykeepahkhay day mahnoa.
I´m missing a suitcase, where can I file a claim?	Me falta una maleta, ¿dónde puedo reclamar?	May fahltah oonah mahlaytah, doanday pwaydoa rayclahmahr?
Here is your boarding pass with all the flight details.	Aquí tiene su tarjeta de embarque con todos los detalles del vuelo.	Ahkee tyaynay soo tahrkhaytah day aymbahrkay kon toadoass loass daytayyayss dayl bhwayloa.

Those suitcases need to be checked in.	*Esas maletas son para facturar.*	*Ausahss mahlaytahss soan pahrah fahktoorahr.*
When we arrive at the airport where we will stop-over, go to the office of the airline.	*A la llegada del aeropuerto de escala preséntese en las oficinas de su compañía.*	*Ah lah yaygahdhah dayl ahayroapwayrtoa day ayskahlah praysayntaysay ayn lahss oafeetheenahss day soo kompahñeeah.*
The plane will make a stop-over in...	*El avión hará escala en...*	*ayl abhyoan ahrah ayskahlah ayn...*
What delay does the flight have?	*¿Qué retraso tiene el vuelo?*	*Kay raytahsoa tyaynay ayl bhwayloa?*
The flight is delayed for..., it has been canceled due to the fog.	*El vuelo sufre un retraso de..., ha sido cancelado por causa de la niebla.*	*Ayl bhwayloa soofray oon raytrahsoa day..., ha seedhoa kahnthaylahdhoa por kahwsah day lah nyaybhlah*
Please take me to terminal number one, international, national.	*Por favor, lléveme a la terminal número 1, internacional, nacional.*	*Por fahbhor, yaybhaymay ah lah taymeenahl noomayroa (1) oonoa, eentaymahthyonahl, nahthyonahl.*

Vocabulario

airport	*aeropuerto*	*ahayroapwayrtoa*
wing	*ala*	*ahlah*
altitude	*altitud*	*ahlteetoodh*
seat	*asiento*	*ahsyayntoa*

landing	aterrizaje	ahtayrreethahkhay
airplane	avión	ahbhyoan
stewardess	azafata	ahthahfahtah
ticket	billete	beeyaytay
booth, cabin	cabina	kahbeenah
seat belt	cinturón de seguridad	theentooroan day saygooreedhahdh
economy class	clase económica	klahsay aykonoameekah
airline company	compañía aérea	konpahñeeah ahayrayah
control of passports	control de pasaportes	kontroal day pahsahpoartayss
take off	despegue	dayspaygway
boarding	embarque	aymbahrkay
emergency	emergencia	aymayrkhaynthyah
luggage	equipaje	aykeephkhay
stop-over	escala	ayskahlah
excess of baggage	exceso de equipaje	ayksthaysoa day aykeepahkhay
arrivals	llegadas	yaygahdhahss
pilot	piloto	peeloatoa
airstrip	pista	peestah
first class	primera clase	preemayrah klahsay
exit	salida	sahleedhah
control tower	torre de control	toarray day kontroal
international flight	vuelo internacional	bhwayloa eentaynahthyonahl
domestic flight	vuelo nacional	bhwayloa nathyonahl

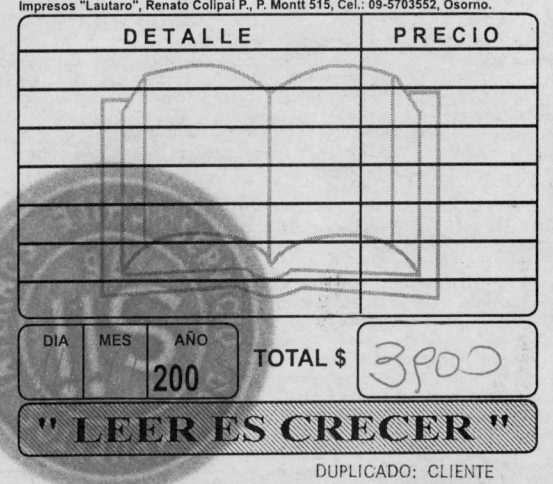

◢▟ULTI◢▖IBROS
LIBRERIA
Mabel Marlene Oyarzún Mansilla
R.U.T.: 9.244.095 - 8
Lord Cochrane Nº 602 - A   -   Fono 247244
Comuna Osorno
E-mail: multilibro@telsur.cl

BOLETA DE VENTA   **Nº   74806**

Impresos "Lautaro", Renato Colipai P., P. Montt 515, Cel.: 09-5703552, Osorno.

DETALLE	PRECIO

DIA	MES	AÑO	TOTAL $	3900
		200		

" LEER ES CRECER "

2.7. Ships, the port

I would like a ticket to...	*Quisiera un pasaje para...*	*Keesyayrah oon pahsahkhay pahrah...*
What day does the ship sail to... and what is it called?	*¿Qué día sale el barco para... y cómo se llama?*	*Kay deeah sahlay ayl bahrkoa pahrah... ee koamoa say yahmah?*
Is there a regular service?	*¿Hay servicio regular?*	*Igh sayrbheethyoa raygoolahr?*
I am dizzy, I need to see a doctor.	*Estoy mareado, tengo necesidad de ver al médico.*	*Aystoi mahrayahdhoa, tayngoa naythayseedhahdh day bhayr ayl maydheekoa.*
Give me a first class cabin, second class, cover.	*Déme un billete, camarote de primera, segunda, cubierta.*	*Daymay oon beeyaytay, kahmahroatay day preemayrah, saygoondhah, koobyayrtah.*
How long is the voyage?	*¿Cuánto tiempo dura la travesía?*	*Kwahntoa tyaympoa doorah lah trahbhayseeah?*
What is the port, the departing dock, boarding... of arrival?	*¿Cuál es el puerto, muelle de salida, embarque... de llegada?*	*Kwahl ayss ayl pwayrtah mwayyay day sahleedhah, aymbahrkay... day yaygahdhah?*
How many and what stops does it make?	*¿Cuántas y qué escalas hace?*	*Kwahntahss ee kay aystkahlahss ahthay?*

Vocabulary

lifeboat	*bote salvavidas*	boatay sahlbhahbheedhahss
cabin	*camarote*	kahmahroatay
captain	*capitán*	kahpeetahn
coast	*costa*	koastah
cruise	*crucero*	kroothayroa
cover	*cubierta*	koobyayrtah
life jacket	*chaleco salvavidas*	chahlaykoa sahlbhahbheedhahss
adrift	*deriva*	dayreebhah
boarding	*embarque*	aymbahrkay
lighthouse	*faro*	fahroa
coast guard	*guardacostas*	gwahrdhahkoastahss
island	*isla*	eeslah
sea	*mar*	mahr
sailor	*marinero*	mahreenayroa
ship doctor	*médico de a bordo*	maydheekoa day ah bordhoa
dock, quay	*muelle*	mwayyay
shipwreck	*naufragio*	nowfrahkhyoa
sailing	*navegación*	nahbhaygahthyon
wave	*ola*	oalah
stern	*popa*	poapah
bow	*proa*	proah
port	*puerto*	pwayrtoa
direction	*rumbo*	roomboa
helm	*timón*	teemoan
transatlantic	*transatlántico*	trahnsahtlahnteekoa
voyage	*travesía*	trahbhayseeah
crew	*tripulación*	treepooahthyon

3. City

3.1. Public transportation

3.1.1. Taxi

Where can I get a taxi?	*¿Dónde puedo tomar un taxi?*	*Doanday pwaydoa toamahr oon tahksee?*
Could you please call me a taxi?	*¿Puede llamarme un taxi, por favor?*	*Pwayday yahmahrmay oon tahksee, por fahbhoar?*
What is the additional fee for luggage, airport, station...?	*¿Cuál es el suplemento de equipaje aeropuerto, estación...?*	*kwahl ayss ayl sooplaymayntoa day aykeepahkhay ahayroapwayrtoa,ays tahthyon...?*
Please take me to this address, to the airport, to the station.	*Lléveme a esta dirección, al aeropuerto, a la estación.*	*Yaybhaymay ah aystah deeraykthyon, ahl ahayroapwayrtoa, ah lah aystahthyon.*
Please stop here.	*¡Pare aquí, por favor!*	*Pahray ahkee,por fahbhoar.*
Could you help me with my luggage?	*¿Podría ayudarme a llevar el equipaje?*	*Poadryah ahyoodahrmay ah yaybhahr ayl aykeepahkhay?*

Could you give me a receipt?	*¿Puede hacerme un recibo?*	Pwayday ahthayrmay oon raytheeboa?
How much do I owe you?	*¿Cuánto le debo?*	Kwahntoa lay dhayboa?
Could you wait for me?	*¿Puede esperarme?*	Pwayday ayspayrahrmay?

3.1.2. Bus

Where does bus number... have a stop?	*El autobús número... ¿dónde tiene la parada?*	Ayl ahwtoabooss noomayroa... doanday tyaynay lah pahrahdhah?
How often does it come by?	*¿Cada cuánto tiempo pasa?*	kahdhah kwahntoa tyaympoa pahsah?
To go to... what bus should I take?	*Para ir a... ¿qué autobús debo tomar?*	Pahrah eer ah... kay ahwtoabooss dhayboa toamahr?
I am in a hurry.	*Tengo prisa.*	Tayngoa preesah
Where is the nearest stop?	*¿Dónde tiene la parada más cercana?*	Doanday tyaynay lah pahrahdhah mahss thayrkahnah?
Could you tell me if this bus stops near...?	*¿Puede decirme si este autobús para cerca de...?*	Pwayde daytheermay see aystay ahwtoabooss pahrah thayrkah day...?

| Could you tell me when we get there? | ¿Me puede avisar cuando lleguemos? | May pwayday abheesahr kwahndoa yaygyaymoass? |
| When do they start running in the morning and when do they stop at night? | ¿A qué hora empiezan a circular por la mañana y hasta qué hora por la noche? | Ah kay oarah aympyaythahn ah theerkoolahr por lah mahñahnah ee ahstah kay oarah por lah noachay? |

3.1.3. Subway

Where is the nearest subway station?	¿Dónde está la estación de metro más cercana?	Doanday aystah lah aystahthyon day maytroa mahss thayrkahnah?
When does the subway start, stop running?	¿A qué hora abre, cierra el metro?	Ah kay oarah ahbray, theerrah ayl maytroa?
How much is the ticket, the coupon?	¿Cuánto cuesta el billete, el bono?	kwahntoa kwaystah ayl beeyaytay, ayl boanoa?
To go to..., what subway line should I take?	Para ir a... ¿qué línea de metro debo tomar?	Pahrah eer ah... kay lenayah day maytroa dayboa toamahr?
In what station should I change trains?	¿En qué estación debo hacer transbordo?	Ayn kay aystahthyon dayboa ahthayr trahnsboardhoa?

3.2. Lodging

3.2.1. Hotel

3.2.1.1 Reception

Good morning, afternoon, evening, do you have any rooms left?	*Buenos días, tardes, noches, ¿quedan habitaciones libres?*	*Bwaynoass deeahs, tahrdayss, noachayss kaydahn ahbeetahthyonsslee brayss?*
Does the hotel have a garage?	*¿Tiene garaje el hotel?*	*Tyaynay gahrahkhay ayl oatayl?*
So, where can I park the car?	*Entonces, ¿dónde puedo aparcar el coche?*	*Ayntoanthayss doanday pwaydoa ahpahrkahr ayl koachay?*
I have the luggage in the trunk.	*Tengo el equipaje en el maletero.*	*Tayngoa ayl aykeepahkhay ayn ayl mahlaytayroa.*
I have a reservation in my name, in ...´s name.	*Tengo reservada una habitación a mi nombre, a nombre de...*	*Tayngoa raysayrbhahdhah oonah habeeahthyon ah mee noambray, ah noambray day...*
Here are the keys, the room is number...	*Aquí tiene usted las llaves, la habitación es la número...*	*Akee tyaynay oostaydh lahss yabhayss, lah ahbeetahthyon ayss lah noomahroa....*

I want a double room, a single room, with a bathroom, for ... days.	*Deseo una habitación doble, individual, con baño, para... días.*	*Daysayoa oonah ahbeetahthyon doablay, eendeebheedwahl, kon bahñoa, pahrah...deeahss.*
Does the room have a telephone?	*¿Tiene teléfono la habitación?*	*tyaynay taylayfoanoa lah ahbeetahthyon?*
How much is the room per day?	*¿Cuál es el precio por día?*	*kwahl ayss ayl praythyoa por deeah?*
Is breakfast included?	*¿Está incluido el desayuno?*	*Aystah eenklweedhoa ayl daysahyoonoa?*
How much is full board, bed and breakfast?	*¿Cuánto cuesta la pensión completa, media pensión?*	*kwahntoa kwaystah lah paynthyon?*
Here is my identification card, my passport.	*Aquí tiene mi carnet de identidad, pasaporte.*	*Ahkee tyaynay mee kahrnayt day eedaynteedhahdh pahsahpoartay*
When should I leave the room?	*¿A qué hora debo dejar la habitación?*	*Ah kay oarah dayboa daykhahr lah ahbeetahthyon?*
Could you give me the key. .?	*¿Puede darme la llave...?*	*Pwayday dahrmay lah yahbhay...?*

Is there any mail for me, any phone messages?	¿Hay correo para mí, algún aviso telefónico?	*Ahy koarrayoa pahrah mee, ahlgoon abheesoa taylayfoaneekoa?*
Could you wake me up at ...?	¿Puede despertarme a las... horas?	*Pwayday dayspayrtahrmay ah lahss... oarahss?*
I will leave tomorrow morning, afternoon, evening.	Me marcharé mañana por la mañana, tarde, noche.	*May mahrchahray mahñahnah por lah mahñahnah, tahrday, noachay*
Could you please get my bill ready?	¿Puede prepararme la cuenta, por favor?	*Pwayday praypahrahrmay lah kwayntah, por fahbhoar?*
Could you tell me what this charge is for?	¿Puede decirme a qué se refiere este concepto?	*Pwayday daytheermay ah kay say rayfyayray aystay konthayptoa?*
Don´t forget to return the keys when you leave the hotel.	No olvide entregar las llaves cuando salga del hotel	*Noa oalbheeday ayntraygahr lahss yahbhayss kwahndoa sahlgah dayl oatayl*
Do you have a storage to leave my luggage until I leave?	¿Tienen consigna para dejar el equipaje hasta mi marcha?	*Tyaynayn konseegnah pahrahdaykhahr aylaykeepahkhay ahstah mee mahrchah?*

Do you take credit cards?	¿Aceptan tarjetas de crédito?	Ahthayptahn tahrkhaytahss day craydeetoa?
Could you send for my luggage?	¿Pueden mandar por mi equipaje?	Pwaydayn mahndahr por mee ekeepakhay?
Could you call a taxi?	¿Pueden llamar a un taxi?	Pwaydaynyahmahr ah oon tahksee?

3.2.1.2. Services

Am I speaking with the bar, restaurant, laundry room, reception?	¿Hablo con el servicio de bar, restaurante, lavandería, recepción?	ahbloa kon ayl sayrbheethyoa day bahr, raystahwrahntay, lahbhahndayryah, raythaypthyon?
I would like you to pick up my pants, shirts to wash, iron.	Deseo que recojan los pantalones, camisas para lavar, planchar.	Daysayoa kay raycoakhahan loass pahntahloanayss, kahmeesahss pahrah lahbhahr, plahnchahr.
I would like you to clean my shoes.	Deseo que me limpien los zapatos.	Daysayoa kay may leempyayn loass thahpahtoass
Does the hotel have a translating service?	¿Tiene el hotel servicio de intérprete?	Tyayay ayl oatayl sayrbheethyoa day eentayrpraytay?

Could you bring me breakfast, a bottle of water, something to eat to my room?	¿Me pueden subir el desayuno, una botella de agua, algo de comer a la habitación?	May pwaydayn soobeer ayl daysahyoonoa, oonah boatayah day agwah, ahlgoa day koamayr ah lah ahbeetahthyon?
I would like you to bring me another bedcover, bath towel...	Quisiera que me subieran otra manta, toalla grande de baño...	Keesyayrah kay may soobyayrahn otra mahntah, toahyah grahnday day bahñoa...
The heating, air conditioning, television, hot water doesn´t work.	La calefacción, aire acondicionado, televisión, agua caliente no funciona.	Lah kahlayfahkthyon, ahyray ahkondeethyonahdh oa, taylaybheethyon, ahgwah kahlyayntay noa foonthyonah.
What time do you serve breakfast, lunch, dinner?	¿A qué hora comienza el servicio de desayunos, comidas, cenas?	Ah kay oarah komyaynthah ayl sayrbhithyoa day daysahyoonoass, komeedhahss, thaynahss?
Where is the bar, the hair salon, the hall, the dining room?	¿Dónde está el bar, la peluquería, el salón, el comedor?	Doanday aystah ayl bahr, lah paylookayryah, ayl sahloan, ayl komaydhoar?

I need paper, envelopes and stamps.	Necesito papel, sobres y sellos.	Naythayseetoa pahpayl, soabrayss ee sayoass
Do you have postcards?	¿Tienen tarjetas postales?	Tyaynayn tahrkhaytahss poastahlayss?
The room is not made up.	La habitación no está arreglada.	Lah ahbeetahthyon noa aystah ahrrayflahdhah.

Vocabulary

bathrobe	albornoz	ahlboarnoath
elevator, lift	ascensor	ahsthaynsoar
bathtub	bañera	bahñayrah
bed	cama	kahmah
waitress	camarera	kahmahrayrah
toothbrush	cepillo de dientes	thaypeeyoa day dyayntayss
no vacancy	completo	komplaytoa
porter	conserje	konsayrkhay
emergency stairway	escalera de emergencia	ayskahlayrah day aymayrkhaynthyah
fire exit	escalera de incendios	ayskahlayrah day eenthayndyoass
faucets	grifos	greefoass
soap	jabón	khahboan
razor	máquina de afeitar	mahkeenah day ahfaytahr
do not disturb	no molestar	noa moalaystahr
toothpaste	pasta dentífrica	pahstah daynteefreekah

comb	*peine*	*paynay*
tip	*propina*	*proapeenah*
complaints	*reclamación*	*rayklahmahthyon*
towel	*toalla*	*toahyah*
slippers	*zapatillas*	*thahpahteeyahss*

3.2.2. Apartments, homes

I wish to rent an apartment, a private home, a country home.	*Deseo alquilar un apartamento, una casa particular, de campo.*	*Daysayoa ahlkeelahr oon ahpahrtahmayntoa, oonah kahsah pahrteekoolahr, day kahmpoa.*
I would like to rent it for... days, ... months.	*Quiero alquilarla por un período de... días, meses...*	*Kyayroa ahlkeelahrlah por oon payryoadhoa day... deeahss, maysayss...*
I will need two, three... in the apartment.	*Necesitaría que el apartamento tenga dos, tres.*	*naythayseetahryah kay ayl ahpahrtahmayntoa tayngah doss, trayss*
Do I need to make a deposit?	*¿Necesito dejar un depósito?*	*naythayseetoa daykhahr oon daypoaseetoa*
Is dinnerware, bed linens, and bath linens included in the rent?	*¿En el alquiler está incluida la vajilla, la ropa de cama, de baño?*	*Ayn ayl ahlkeelayr aystah eenklweedhah lah bhahkheeyah, lah roapah day kahmah, day bahñoa?*

Does it have appliances?	*¿Tienen todos los electrodomés-ticos?*	*Tyaynayn toadoss loass aylayktroadoamay steekoass?*
Is the water, light, heating included in the rent?	*En el alquiler ¿está incluido el consumo de agua, luz, calefacción, otros?*	*Ayn ayl alkeelayr aystah eenklwedhoa ayl konsoomoa day ahgwah, looth, kahlayfahkthyon. oatroass?*
I would like the apartment to be oceanside.	*Quisiera que el apartamento estuviera en primera línea de playa.*	*keesyayrah kay ayl ahpahrtahmayntoa aystoobhyayrah ayn preemayrah leenayah day plahyah.*
I would like the apartment to be in a quiet area.	*Quisiera que el apartamento no fuera ruidoso.*	*Keesyayrah kay ayl ahpahrtahmayntao noa fwayrah rweedhoasoa.*
Does the apartment have a pool? Is there a playground for children?	*¿Tiene el apartamento piscina? ¿Y zona de recreo para los niños?*	*Tyaynay ayl ahpahrtahmayntao peestheenah? Ee thoanah day raycrayoa pahrah loass neeñoass?*

Vocabulary

rent	*alquiler*	*ahlkeelayr*
furnished	*amueblado*	*ahmwayblahdhoa*
closet	*armario ropero*	*ahrmahryoa roapayroa*

attic	*buhardilla*	*booahrdeeyah*
heating	*calefacción*	*kahlayfahkthyon*
kitchen	*cocina*	*koatheenah*
dining room	*comedor*	*komaydhoar*
contract	*contrato*	*kontrahtoa*
bathroom	*cuarto de baño*	*kwahrtoa day bahñoa*
decoration	*decoración*	*daykoarahthyon*
bedroom	*dormitorio*	*dhoarmeetoaryoa*
shower	*ducha*	*doochah*
garage	*garaje*	*gahrahkhay*
room	*habitación*	*ahbeetahthyon*
garden	*jardín*	*hahrdeen*
washer	*lavadora*	*lahbhahdoarah*
dishwasher	*lavavajillas*	*lahbhahbhahkheeyahss*
microwave	*microondas*	*meekroondhahss*
corridor	*pasillo*	*pahseeyoa*
backyard	*patio*	*pahtyoa*
floor	*piso*	*peesoa*
first floor	*planta baja*	*plahntah bahkhah*
portal	*portal*	*poartahl*
door	*puerta*	*pwayrtah*
for rent	*se alquila*	*say ahlkeelah*
basement	*sótano*	*soatahnoa*
ceiling	*techo*	*taychoa*
roof	*tejado*	*taykhahdhoa*
television	*televisión*	*taylaybheethyon*
window	*ventana*	*bhentahnah*
housing	*vivienda*	*bheebhyaydhah*
dishes	*vajilla*	*bhahkheeyah*

3.2.3. Camping

Do you have a camping guide?	¿Tienen ustedes una guía de campings?	*Tyaynayn oostaydayss oonah geeah day kahmpeengss?*
Is there a place to camp near here?	¿Hay algún camping cerca de aquí?	*Ahy ahlgoon kampeeng thayrkah day ahkee?*
How much is camping per day, per tent, per caravan, per car?	¿Cuál es el precio de acampada por día, para tienda, para caravana, para coche?	*Kwahl ayss ayl praythyoa day ahkampahdhah por deeah, pahrah tyayndhah, pahrah kahrahbhahnah, pahrah koachay?*
Do you have sites with electric connections and drinkable water?	¿Existen parcelas con toma de electricidad y agua potable?	*Aykseestayn pahrthaylahss kon toamah day aylayktreetheedha hdh ee agwah poatahblay?*
Can we camp here?	¿Podemos acampar aquí?	*Pwdaymoass ahkahmpahr hkee?*
Where are the showers, the restrooms, toilets?	¿Dónde están la ducha, los servicios?	*Doanday aystahn lah doochah, loass sayrbheethyoass?*
Is there a supermarket near here?	¿Hay algún supermercado cerca de aquí?	*Ahy ahlgoon soopayrmayrkahdh oa thayrkah day ahkee?*

Vocabulary

can opener	*abrelatas*	*Ahbraylahtahss*
guest house	*albergue*	*ahlbayrgway*
gas tubes	*bombona de gas*	*boamboanah day gahss*
emergency kit	*botiquín*	*boateekeen*
bar	*cafetería*	*kahfaytayryah*
layaway bed	*cama plegable*	*kahmah playgahblay*
canteen	*cantina*	*kahnteeenah*
camping stove	*hornillo portátil*	*oarneeyoa poartahteel*
flashlight	*linterna*	*leentayrnah*
shelter	*refugio*	*rayfookhyoa*
corkscrew	*sacacorchos*	*sahkahkoarchoass*
sleeping bag	*saco de dormir*	*sahkoa day doarmeer*
fold out chair	*silla plegable*	*seeyah playgahblay*
thermos	*termo*	*tayrmoa*
tent	*tienda de campaña*	*tyaydhah day kampahñah*

3.3. Food

3.3.1. Restaurants

Where can you eat well, cheap?	*¿Dónde se puede comer bien, barato?*	*Doanday say pwayday komayr byayn, bahrahtoa?*
Could we take this table?	*¿Podemos ocupar esta mesa?*	*Poadaymoass oakoopahr aystah maysah?*

We would like to make a reservation for a table for... and for... people.	*Desearíamos reservar una mesa para las... horas y para... personas.*	*Daysayahryahmoas s raysayrbhahr oonah maysah pahrah lahss... oarahs ee pahrah... payrsoanahss.*
A table near the window, set apart, without much noise.	*Una mesa junto a la ventana, aislada, sin ruido.*	*Oonah maysah hoontoa ah lah bhayntahnah, ahyslahdhah, seen rweedhoa.*
Without salt, sauce, lightly salted, well done, medium rare, medium.	*Sin sal, salsa, poco salado, muy hecho, poco hecho, en su punto.*	*Seen sahl, sahlsah, poakoa sahlahdhoa, mwee aychoa, poakoa aychoa, ayn soo poontoa.*
Waiter, please, an aperitif.	*Camarero, por favor, un vino de aperitivo.*	*Kahmahrayroa, por fahbhoar, oon bheeno day ahpayreeteebhoa*
Waiter, serve us the special of the day!	*Camarero, ¡sírvanos el menú del día!*	*kahmahrayroa, seerbhahnoass aylmaynoo dayl deeah*
Let me have the menu, please.	*Deme la carta, por favor.*	*Daymay lah cahrtah, por fahbhoar*
Please bring us wine from this country, this area, house wine, water.	*Tráiganos vino del país, de esta región, de la casa, agua.*	*Trahygahnoass bheenoa dayl pahyss, day aystah raykhyoan, day lah kahsah agwah.*

Do you have any vegetarian dishes?	¿Tienen platos vegetarianos?	Tyaynayn plahtoass bhaykhaytahryahnoass?
I want something quick, we're in a hurry.	Quisiera algo ligero, tenemos prisa.	Keesyayrah ahlgoa leekhayroa, taynaymoass preesah.
Could you recommend something to eat, something typical of this area?	Aconséjenos qué podemos comer, un menú típico de esta región.	Ahkonsaykhaynoass kay podaymoass komayr, oon maynoo teepeekoa day aystah raykhyoan.
That is enough, thank you.	Suficiente, gracias.	Soofeethyaytay, grahthyahs
What kind of cheeses do you have?	¿Qué clase de quesos tienen?	Kay klahsay day kaysoass tyaynayn?
What is the house speciality?	¿Cuál es la especialidad de la casa?	kwahl ayss lah ayspaythyahleedhadh day lah kahsah?
What wine would you suggest we order?	¿Qué vino nos aconseja que tomemos?	kay bheenoa noass ahkonsaykhah kay toamaymoass?
I would like some more, please.	Desearía un poco más, por favor.	Daysayahryah oon poakoa mahss, por fahbhoar.

| Without condiments, we'll add them. | *Sin condimentar, nosotros lo añadiremos.* | *Seen kondeemayntahr, noasoatroass loa ahñahdeeraymoass* |

3.3.1.1. The table — Vocabulary

sugar caddy	*azucarero*	*ahthookahrayroa*
tray	*bandeja*	*bahndaykhah*
bottle	*botella*	*boatayah*
coffeepot	*cafetera*	*kahfaytayrah*
ashtray	*cenicero*	*thayneethayroa*
glass	*copa*	*koapah*
spoon	*cuchara*	*koochahrah*
small spoon	*cucharilla*	*koochahreeyah*
knife	*cuchillo*	*koocheeyoa*
table cloth	*mantel*	*mahntayl*
menu	*menú*	*maynoo*
table	*mesa*	*maysah*
toothpicks	*palillos*	*pahleeyoass*
bread	*pan*	*pahn*
soup plate	*plato sopero*	*plahtoa soapayroa*
deep	*hondo*	*oandhoa*
flat	*llano*	*yahnoa*
corkscrew	*sacacorchos*	*sahkahkoarchoass*
saltcellar	*salero*	*sahlahroa*
tureen	*salsera*	*sahlsayrah*
napkin	*servilleta*	*sayrbheeyaytah*
soup tureen	*sopera*	*soapayrah*
small cup	*tacita*	*tahtheetah*
cup	*taza*	*tahthah*

fork	*tenedor*	*Taynaydhoar*
teapot	*tetera*	*taytayrah*
glass	*vaso*	*bhahsoa*
vinegar bottles	*vinagreras*	*bheenahgrayrahss*

3.3.1.2. Condiments and spices — Vocabulary

oil	*aceite*	*Athaytay*
garlic	*ajo*	*ahkhoa*
saffron	*azafrán*	*ahthahfrahn*
bechamel	*bechamel*	*baychahmayl*
cinnamon	*canela*	*kahnaylah*
hot pepper	*guindilla*	*geendeeyah*
fennel	*hinojo*	*eenoakhoa*
laurel	*laurel*	*lahwrayl*
butter	*mantequilla*	*mahntaykeeyah*
margarine	*margarina*	*mahrgahreenah*
mayonnaise	*mayonesa*	*mahyoanaysah*
mustard	*mostaza*	*moastahthah*
cream	*nata*	*nahtah*
oregano	*orégano*	*oaraygahnoa*
parsley	*perejil*	*payraykheel*
pepper	*pimienta*	*peemyayntah*
salt	*sal*	*sahl*
sauce	*salsa*	*sahlsah*
vinegar	*vinagre*	*bheenahgray*

3.3.1.3. Flavor and quality food — Vocabulary

| acid | *ácido* | *ahtheedhoa* |
| bitter | *amargo* | *ahmahrgoa* |

good	*bueno*	*bhwaynoa*
hot	*caliente*	*kahlyayntay*
sweet	*dulce*	*dhoolthay*
hard	*duro*	*dooroa*
fresh	*fresco*	*frayskoa*
cold	*frío*	*freeoa*
light	*ligero*	*leekhayroa*
heavy	*pesado*	*paysahdhoa*
spicy	*picante*	*peekahntay*
delicious	*rico*	*teekoa*
strong flavor, taste	*sabor fuerte*	*sahboar fwayrtay*
flavorful, tasty	*sabroso*	*sahbroasoa*
salted	*salado*	*sahlahdhoa*
flat	*soso*	*soasoa*
soft	*suave*	*swahbhay*
temperate	*templado*	*taymplahdhoa*
lukewarm	*tibio*	*teebyoa*
tender	*tierno*	*tyernoa*

3.3.1.4. The kitchen: elaboration   Vocabulary

smoked	*ahumado*	*Ahoomahdhoa*
just right, medium	*al punto*	*ahl poontoa*
grilled	*asado*	*ahsahdhoa*
well done	*bien hecho*	*byayn aychoa*
cooked	*cocido*	*koatheedhoa*
frosted	*congelado*	*konkhaylahdhoa*
raw	*crudo*	*croodhoa*
breaded	*empanado*	*aympahnahdhoa*

thick	*espeso*	*ayspaysoa*
stew	*estofado*	*aystoafahdhoa*
fried	*frito*	*freetoa*
stewed	*guisado*	*geesahdhoa*
boiled	*hervido*	*ayrbheedhoa*
grilled	*parrilla*	*pahrreeyah*
grill	*plancha*	*plahnchah*
medium rare	*poco hecho*	*poakoa aychoa*
breaded	*rebozado*	*rayboathahdhoa*
stuffed	*relleno*	*rayyaynoa*
salted	*salteado*	*sahltayahdhoa*

3.3.2. Food — Vocabulary

olives	*aceitunas*	*Ahthaytoonahss*
sausage	*chorizo*	*choareethoa*
salads	*ensaladas*	*aynsahlahdhahss*
potato salad	*ensaladilla rusa*	*aynsahlahdheeyah toosah*
side dish	*entremeses*	*ayntraymaysayss*
cold cuts	*fiambres*	*fyahmbrayss*
dry fruit	*frutos secos*	*frootoass saykoass*
salted crackers	*galletas saladas*	*gahyaytahss sahlahdhahss*
york ham	*jamón de york*	*khahmoan day yoark*
serrano ham	*jamón serrano*	*khahmoan sayrrahnoa*
sausage	*morcilla*	*moartheeyah*
french fries	*patatas fritas*	*pahtahtahss freetahss*
pates	*patés*	*pahtayss*
sausage	*salchichón*	*sahlcheechoan*
smoked salmon	*salmón ahumado*	*sahlmoan a hoomahdhoa*

Soups	*Sopas*	*Soups*
consommé	*consomé*	*Konsoamay*
chicken stock	*caldo de ave*	*kahldhoa day ahbhay*
meat soup	*sopa de carne*	*soapah day kahrnay*
vegetable soup	*de verduras*	*day bhayrdhoorahss*
rice soup	*de arroz*	*day ahrroath*
noodle soup	*de fideos*	*day feedhayoass*
onion soup	*de cebolla*	*day thayboayah*
fish soup	*de pescado*	*day payscahdhoa*

Pasta	*Pasta*	*Pasta*
canneloni	*canelones*	*kanayloanayss*
spaghetti	*espaguetis*	*ayspahgwayteess*
lasagne	*lasaña*	*lahsahñah*
macaroni	*macarrones*	*mahkahrroanayss*
ravióli	*raviolis*	*rahbhyoaleess*

Vegetables	*Verduras*	*Vegetables*
cabbage	*acelga*	*ahthaylgah*
artichokes	*alcachofas*	*ahlkahchoafahss*
celery	*apio*	*ahpyoa*
eggplants	*berenjenas*	*bayraynkhaynahss*
broccoli	*brécoles*	*braykoalayss*
zucchinni	*calabacín*	*kahlahbahtheen*
pumpkin	*calabaza*	*kahlahbahthah*
onions	*cebollas*	*thayboayahss*
cabbage	*col*	*koal*
brussels sprouts	*coles de bruselas*	*koalayss day broosaylahss*
mushrooms	*champiñones*	*chahmpeeñoanayss*

endives	*endivias*	*ayndeebhyahss*
escarole	*escarola*	*ayskahroalah*
asparagus	*espárragos*	*ayspahrrahgoass*
spinach	*espinaca*	*ayspeenahkah*
peas	*guisantes*	*gweesahntayss*
green beans	*judías verdes*	*khoodeeahs bhayrdayss*
lettuce	*lechuga*	*laychoogah*
potatoes	*patatas*	*pahtahtahss*
cucumber	*pepino*	*paypeenoa*
peppers	*pimientos*	*peemyayntoass*
leeks	*puerros*	*pwayrroass*
radishes	*rábanos*	*rahbahnoass*
beet	*remolacha*	*raymoalahchah*
mushrooms	*setas*	*saytahss*
tomatoes	*tomates*	*tomahtayss*
carrot	*zanahoria*	*thahnahoaryah*
Beans	*Legumbres*	*Beans*
chickpeas	*garbanzos*	*gahrbahnthoass*
beans	*judías*	*khoodeeahss*
lentils	*lentejas*	*layntaykhahss*
Eggs	*Huevos*	*Eggs*
baked	*al plato*	*ahl plahtoa*
hard boiled	*duros*	*dooroass*
poached	*escalfados*	*ayskahlfahdhoass*
fried	*fritos*	*freetoass*
boiled	*pasados por agua*	*pahsahdhoass por agwah*
scrambled	*revueltos*	*raybhwayltoass*
deviled	*rellenos*	*rayyaynoass*
omelette	*tortilla*	*toarteeyah*

Fish	*Pescados*	*Pescados*
anchovy	*anchoa*	*ahnchoah*
herring	*arenque*	*ahraynkay*
tuna	*atún*	*ahtoon*
cod	*bacalao*	*bahkahlahoa*
sea bream	*besugo*	*baysoogoa*
fresh anchovy	*boquerón*	*boakayroan*
mackerel	*caballa*	*kahbahyah*
rooster	*gallo*	*gahyoa*
sole	*lenguado*	*layngwahdhoa*
sea bass	*lubina*	*loobeenah*
hake	*merluza*	*mayrloothah*
grouper	*mero*	*mayroa*
whiting	*pescadilla*	*payskahdeeyah*
sword fish	*pez espada*	*payth ayspahdha*
angler	*rape*	*rahpay*
turbot	*rodaballo*	*roadhahbahyoa*
salmon	*salmón*	*sahlmoan*
sardine	*sardina*	*sahrdeenah*
trout	*trucha*	*troochah*
grilled	*a la plancha*	*ah lah plahnchah*
marinated	*marinados*	*mahreenahdoass*
salted	*a la sal*	*ah lah sahl*
fried	*fritos*	*freetoas*
in sauce	*en salsa*	*ayn sahlsah*
Shellfish	*Mariscos*	**Shellfish**
clams	*almejas*	*ahlmaykhahss*
elver	*angula*	*ahngoolah*

City

cockle	*berberecho*	*bayrbayraychoa*
lobster	*bogavante*	*boagahbhahntay*
squids	*calamares*	*kahlahmahrayss*
crab	*cangrejo*	*kahngraykhoa*
spider crab	*centolla*	*thayntoayah*
norway lobster	*cigala*	*theegahlah*
shrimps	*gambas*	*gahmbahss*
lobster	*langosta*	*lahngoastah*
prawn	*langostino*	*lahngoasteenoa*
mussels	*mejillones*	*maykheeyoanayss*
razor clam	*navaja*	*nahbhahkhah*
oysters	*ostras*	*oastrahss*
octopus	*pulpo*	*poolpao*
cuttlefish	*sepia*	*saypyah*
Wild game and birds	*Caza y aves*	*Wild game and birds*
gelding	*capón*	*kahpoan*
partridge	*codorniz*	*kodoarneeth*
rabbit	*conejo*	*konaykhoa*
roedeer	*corzo*	*korthoa*
pheasant	*faisán*	*fahsahn*
hen	*gallina*	*gahyeenah*
goose	*ganso*	*gahnsoa*
boar	*jabalí*	*khahbahlee*
hare	*liebre*	*lyaybray*
duck	*pato*	*pahtoa*
turkey	*pavo*	*pahbhoa*
chicken	*pollo*	*poayoa*
deer	*venado*	*bhaynahdhoa*

Meats	Carnes	Meats
ox	*buey*	*bway*
pig	*cerdo*	*thayrdoa*
lamb	*cordero*	*kordayroa*
veal	*ternera*	*tayrnayrah*
bacon	*tocino*	*toatheenoa*
cow	*vaca*	*bhahkah*
Roasted and stews	*Asados y guisos*	**Roasted and stews**
meatballs	*albóndigas*	*ahlboandeegahss*
roasted	*asados*	*ahsahdhoass*
chopped meat	*carne picada*	*cahrnay peekahdhah*
baby back ribs	*costillas de cerdo*	*kosteeyahss day thayrdhoa*
lambchop	*chuleta de cordero*	*choolaytah day kordayroa*
porkchop	*de cerdo*	*choolaytoan day bway*
T-bone steak	*chuletón de buey*	*day thayrdhoa*
escalope	*escalope*	*ayskahloapay*
stew	*estofado*	*aystoafahdhoa*
fillet	*filete*	*feelaytay*
breaded fillet	*filete empanado*	*feelaytay aympahnahdhoa*
meat stew	*guiso de carne*	*gweesoa day kahrnay*
hamburger	*hamburguesa*	*ahmboorgwaysah*
liver	*hígado*	*eegahdhoa*
tongue	*lengua*	*layngwah*
loin	*lomo*	*loamoa*
thigh	*muslo*	*moosloa*
leg of lamb	*pierna de cordero*	*pyayrnah day kordayroa*

City

kidney	*riñones*	*reeñoanayss*
brains	*sesos*	*saysoass*
sirloin	*solomillo*	*soaloameeyoa*

3.3.2.2. Fruits and desserts   Vocabulary

Cheeses	*Quesos*	*Cheeses*
sheep	*de oveja*	*day oabhaykhah*
from cow´s milk	*de vaca*	*day bhahkah*
from goat´s milk	*de cabra*	*day kahbrah*
curd cheese	*requesón*	*raykaysoan*
cured cheese	*queso curado*	*kaysoa koorahdhoa*
semicured	*semicurado*	*saymeekoorahdhoa*
tender	*tierno*	*tyaynoa*
blue	*azul*	*ahthool*
melted cheese	*queso fundido*	*kaysoa foondheedhoa*
fresh	*fresco*	*frayskoa*
Dry fruits	*Frutos secos*	*Dry fruits*
almonds	*almendras*	*ahlmayndrahss*
hazel-nuts	*avellanas*	*abhayyahnahss*
chestnuts	*castañas*	*kahstahñahss*
nuts	*nueces*	*nwaythayss*
pine nuts	*piñones*	*peeñoanayss*
sunflower seeds	*pipas de girasol*	*peepahss day kheerahsoal*
pistachios	*pistachos*	*peestahchoass*
Fruits	*Frutas*	*Fruits*
avocados	*aguacates*	*agwahkahtayss*

apricots	*albaricoques*	*ahlbahreekokayss*
cherries	*cerezas*	*thayraythahss*
plums	*ciruelas*	*theerwaylahss*
coconuts	*cocos*	*Koakoass*
dates	*dátiles*	*dahteelayss*
raspberries	*frambuesas*	*frahmbwaysahss*
strawberries	*fresas*	*fraysahss*
figs	*higos*	*eegoass*
kiwi	*kiwi*	*keewee*
lemons	*limones*	*leemoanayss*
mandarin	*mandarinas*	*mahndahreenahss*
mango	*mango*	*mahngoa*
apples	*manzanas*	*mahnthahnahss*
peaches	*melocotones*	*maylokoatoanayss*
melons	*melones*	*mayloanayss*
quince	*membrillo*	*maymbreeyoa*
blueberries	*moras*	*moarahss*
oranges	*naranjas*	*nahrahnkhahss*
pears	*peras*	*payrahss*
pineapples	*piñas*	*peñahss*
bananas	*plátanos*	*plahtahnoass*
grapefruit	*pomelo*	*poamaylao*
watermelons	*sandías*	*sahndeeahss*
grapes	*uvas*	*oobhahss*
Sweet and desserts	***Dulces y postres***	***Sweets and desserts***
pudding	*budín*	*boodeen*
cream	*crema*	*craymah*
custard	*flan*	*flahn*
ice cream	*helado*	*aylahdhoa*

marmalade	*mermelada*	*mayrmaylahdhah*
honey	*miel*	*myayl*
cream	*nata*	*nahtah*
cake	*pastel*	*pahstayl*
tart	*tarta*	*tahrtah*
yogurt	*yogur*	*yoagoor*
Pastries	***Bollería***	***Pastries***
cake	*bizcocho*	*beethkoachoa*
chocolates	*bombones*	*boamboanayss*
bun	*bollo*	*boayao*
cookies	*galletas*	*gahyaytahss*
puff pastry	*hojaldre*	*oakhahldray*
cookies	*pastas*	*pahstahss*
meringue	*merengue*	*mayrayngway*
Bread	***Pan***	***Bread***
rye bread	*de centeno*	*day thayntaynoa*
wheat	*de trigo*	*day treegoa*
quick bread	*de molde*	*day moalday*
fresh	*fresco*	*frayskoa*
whole	*integral*	*eentayfrahl*
grated	*rallado*	*rahyahdhoa*
without salt	*sin sal*	*seen sahl*
roll	*panecillo*	*pahnaytheeyoa*

3.3.3. Drinks — Vocabulary

Water	***Agua***	***Water***
mineral	*mineral*	*meenayrahl*
sparkling	*con gas*	*kon gahss*
tap, mineral	*sin gas*	*seen gahss*
tap	*del grifo*	*dayl greefoa*

bottled	embotellada	aymboatayyahdhah
tonic	tónica	toaneekah
Coffee	*Café*	*Coffee*
black	solo	soaloa
with a little milk	cortado	coartahdhoa
decaffeinated	descafeinado	dayskahfayynahdhoa
with ice	con hielo	kon yayloa
espresso	exprés	ayksprayss
short	corto	coartoa
long	largo	lahrgoa
with milk	con leche	kon laychay
without sugar	sin azúcar	seen ahthookahr
with sugar	con azúcar	kon ahthookahr
Tea	*Té*	*Tea*
with lemon	con limón	kon leemoan
with milk	con leche	kon laychay
with toast and butter	con tostadas y mantequilla	kon toastahdhahss ee mahntaykeeyah
with honey	con miel	kon myayl
Beer	*Cerveza*	*Beer*
lager	rubia	roobyah
black	negra	naygrah
Wine	*Vino*	*Wine*
white wine	vino blanco	bheenoa blahnkoa
red	tinto	teentoa
rose	rosado	roasahdhoa
dry	seco	saykoa
sweet	dulce	doolthay
room temperature	del tiempo	dayl tyaympoa
cold	frío	freeoa

Juices	*Zumos*	*Juices*
orange	*de naranja*	*day nahrahnkhah*
grapefruit	*de pomelo*	*day poamayloa*
lemon	*de limón*	*day leemoan*
tomato	*de tomate*	*day toamahtay*
Other drinks	**Otras bebidas**	*Other drinks*
chocolate	*chocolate*	*choakoalahtay*
soda	*gaseosa*	*gahsayoasah*
gin	*ginebra*	*kheenaybrah*
rum	*ron*	*roan*
liquor	*licor*	*leekoar*
milk	*leche*	*laychay*
lemonade	*limonada*	*leemoanahdha*
infusions	*infusiones*	*eenfoothyonss*
soda	*soda*	*soadhah*
anisette	*anís*	*ahneess*

3.3.4. Cafetería and bar

Waiter, may I have a coffee with milk.	*Camarero, ¡póngame un café con leche...!*	*Kahmahrayroa, poangahmay oon kahfay kon laychay....!*
What will you have to drink?	*¿Qué van a tomar?*	*Kay bhahn ah toamahr?*
I will have a..., serve me a...	*Yo tomaré..., sírvame...*	*Yo toamahray...., seerbhahmay....*
Give me a little more...	*Déme un poco más de...*	*Daymay oon poakoa mahss day....*

98

Will you please bring me the menu?	*¿Me hace el favor de traerme la lista de precios?*	*May ahthay ayl fahbhoar day trahayrmay lah leestah day praytheeoass?*
Where is the public phone?	*¿Dónde está la cabina telefónica?*	*Doanday aystah lah kahbeenah taylayfoaneekah?*
Where are the restrooms, toilets?	*¿Dónde están los lavabos?*	*Doaday aystahn loass lahbhahboass?*
How much do I owe you?	*¿Cuánto le debo?*	*Kwahntoa lay dayboa?*

City

Vocabulary

appetizer	*aperitivo*	*ahpayreeteebhoa*
tray	*bandeja*	*bahndaykhah*
bar	*bar*	*bahr*
coffeepot	*cafetera*	*kahfaytayrah*
beer	*cerveza*	*thayrbhaythah*
draft beer	*cerveza de barril*	*thayrbhaythah day bahrreel*
gin	*ginebra*	*kheenaybrah*
ice	*hielo*	*yayloa*
liquor	*licor*	*leekoar*
counter	*mostrador*	*moastrahdhoar*
soft drink	*refresco*	*rayfrayskoa*
juice	*zumo*	*thoomoa*

3.4. Shopping

3.4.1. Gifts, handicrafts

I would like to see if I can find something I like to take it as a souvenir.	*Quisiera ver si encuentro algo que me guste para llevármelo de recuerdo.*	*Keesyayrah bhayr see aynkwayntroa ahlgoa kay may goostay pahrah yaybhahrmayloa day raykwayrdhoa.ç*
I would like to buy crafts.	*Deseo comprar algún objeto de artesanía.*	*Daysayoa komprahr algoon oabkhaytoa day ahrtaysahneeah*
What is the price of this statue, painting, craft...?	*¿Qué precio tiene esta figura, cuadro, manualidad...?*	*Kay praythyoa tyaynay aystah feegoorah, kwahdhroa, mahnwahleedhadh...?*
Is this ceramic typical of this area?	*¿Esta cerámica es típica de esta región?*	*Aystah thayrahmeekah ayll teepeekah day aystah raykhyoan?*
What crafts are typical from this area?	*¿Qué otra artesanía típica tienen?*	*Kay oatrah ahrtaysahneeah teepeekah tyaynayn.*
Let me have these postcards.	*Déme esta colección de tarjetas postales.*	*Dayme aystah kolaykthyon day tahrkhaytahss poastahlayss.*

City

Vocabulary

tray	*bandeja*	*bahndaykhah*
wallet	*billetero*	*beeyaytayroa*
embroidery	*bordado*	*boardhahdhoa*
portfolio	*cartera*	*kahrtayrah*
ashtray	*cenicero*	*thayneethayroa*
ceramic	*cerámica*	*thayrahmeekah*
belt	*cinturón*	*theentooroan*
tie	*corbata*	*koarbahtah*
crystal	*cristal*	*kreestahl*
lace	*encajes*	*aynkahkhayss*
vase	*florero*	*floarayroa*
toy	*juguete*	*khoogwaytay*
key ring	*llavero*	*yahbhayroa*
cloth	*mantel*	*mahntayl*
doll	*muñeca*	*mooñaykah*
handkerchief	*pañuelo*	*pahñwayloa*
umbrella	*paraguas*	*pahrahgwahss*
cigarrette case	*pitillera*	*peeteeyayrah*
porcelain	*porcelana*	*poarthaylahnah*

City

3.4.2. Stores

Where is the shopping center, the supermarket, the store...?	*¿Dónde está el centro comercial, mercado, tienda...?*	*Doanday aystah ayl thaytroa komayrthyahl, mayrcahdhoa, tyayndha...?*
How can I get there?	*¿Cómo puedo ir allí?*	*Koamao pwaydhao eer ahyee?*

Are there any department stores around here?	¿Hay algunos grandes almacenes cerca de aquí?	Ahy ahlgoonoass grahndayss ahlmahthaynayss thayrkah day ahkee?
Good morning, afternoon, I would like to buy...	Buenos días, buenas tardes, quisiera comprar...	Bwaynoass deeahss, bwaynahss tahrdayss, keesyayrah komprahr...
I would like to try it on.	Desearía probármelo	Daysayahreeah proabahrmayloa
Could you show me something else?	¿Puede enseñarme algo más?	Pwayday aynsayñahrmay ahlgoa mahss
How much is it?	¿Cuánto cuesta?	kwahntoa kwaystah?
Do you have anything less expensive?	¿No tiene algo más económico?	Noa tyaynay ahlgoa mahss aykonoameekoa?
I don't like it, I like it very much, but it's too expensive.	No me gusta, me gusta mucho, pero es muy caro.	Noa may goostah, may goostah moochoa, payroa ayss mwee kahroa.
I'll take it, do you accept credit cards.	Me lo llevo, ¿aceptan ustedes tarjetas de crédito?	May loa yaybhoa, athayptahn oostaydayss tahrkhaytahss day kraydheetoa?

| I would like to exchange this article of clothing, this thing. Here is the receipt. | *Desearía cambiar esta prenda, objeto. Aquí está el recibo.* | *Daysayahreeah kahmbyahr aystah prayndhah, oabkhaytoa. Ahkee aystah ayl raytheeboa.* |
| Where can I find an umbrella? | *¿Dónde puedo encontrar un paraguas?* | *Doanday pwaydoa aynkontrahr oon pahrahgwahss?* |

Vocabulary

carpets	*alfombras*	*ahlfoambrahss*
antiques	*antigüedades*	*ahnteegwaydhahdhayss*
housewares	*artículos del hogar*	*ahrteekooloass dayl oagahr*
exchange	*cambiar*	*kambyahr*
buy	*comprar*	*komprahr*
glassware	*cristalería*	*creestahlayreeah*
clerk	*dependiente*	*daypayndyayntay*
return	*devolver*	*daybhoalbhayr*
disks	*discos*	*deeskoass*
choose	*elegir*	*aylaykheer*
window	*escaparate*	*ayskahpahrahtay*
spend	*gastar*	*gahstahr*
schedule	*horario*	*oarahryoa*
toys	*juguetes*	*khoogwaytayss*
furniture	*muebles*	*mwayblayss*
newspapers	*periódicos*	*payryoadeekoass*
try on	*probar*	*proabahr*

gifts	*regalos*	*raygahloass*
clocks	*relojes*	*rayloakhayss*
clothes	*ropa*	*roapah*
knits	*tejidos*	*taykheedhoass*
salesman	*vendedor*	*bhayndhaydhoar*
shoes	*zapatos*	*thahpahtoass*

3.4.2.1. Florist shop

I would like an arrangement of flowers...	*Quisiera un ramo de flores...*	*Keesyayrah oon rahmoa day floarayss...*
What are these flowers called?	*¿Cómo se llaman estas flores?*	*Koamoa say yahmahn aystahs floarayss?*
I would like this centerpiece, this pot of...	*Desearía este centro, maceta de...*	*Daysayahreeah aystay thaytroa, mahthaytah day...*
Can you send these flowers to this address?	*¿Puede mandar este ramo de flores a esta dirección?*	*Pwayday mahndhahr aystay rahmoa day floarayss ah aystah deeraykthyon?*
Send it this afternoon, tomorrow morning.	*Mándelo para esta tarde, mañana por la mañana.*	*mahndayloa pahrah aystah tahrday, mahñahnah por lah mahñahnah. ahthahlayah*

Vocabulary

English	Spanish	Pronunciation
azalea	*azalea*	*ahthahlayah*
lily	*azucena*	*ahthoothaynah*
camellia	*camelia*	*kahmaylyah*
carnation	*clavel*	*klahbhayl*
chrysanthemum	*crisantemo*	*kreesahntaymoa*
dahlia	*dalia*	*dahlyah*
flower	*flor*	*floar*
florist	*florista*	*floareestah*
flower shop	*floristería*	*floareestayreeah*
gardenia	*gardenia*	*gahrdaynyah*
geranium	*geranio*	*khayrahnyoa*
leaf	*hoja*	*oakhah*
hydrangea	*hortensia*	*oartaynsyah*
hyacinth	*jacinto*	*khahtheentoa*
jasmine	*jazmín*	*khahthmeen*
lilacs	*lilas*	*leelahss*
iris	*lirio*	*leeryoa*
pot	*maceta*	*mahthaytah*
magnolia	*magnolia*	*mahgnoalyah*
daisy	*margarita*	*mahrgahreetah*
narcissus	*narciso*	*mahrtheesoa*
orchid	*orquídea*	*oarkeedhayah*
plant	*planta*	*plahntah*
arrangement	*ramo*	*rahmoa*
rose	*rosa*	*roasah*
tulip	*tulipán*	*tooleepahn*
violet	*violeta*	*bhyoalaytah*

3.4.2.2. Photography

I would like to have some passport pictures taken.	*Deseo que me haga unas fotos para el pasaporte.*	*Dayayoa kay may ahgha oonahss foatoas pahrah ayl pahsahpoartay.*
Give me a roll of color film, brand name... of twenty-four, thirty-six pictures.	*Deme un carrete de color, marca... de 24, 36, fotografías.*	*Daymay oon kahrraytay day koaloar, mahrkah... day (24) bhaytay kwatroa, (36) trayntah sayss foatoagrahfeeahss.*
I would like this roll of film developed matte, glossy, when will it be ready?	*Quisiera revelar este carrete de fotos en mate, en brillo, ¿para cuándo estará?*	*Keesyayrah raybhaylahr aystay kahrraytay day foatoass ayn mahtay, ayn breeyoa, pahrah kwahndoa aystahrah?*
I would like some copies made of these pictures and an enlargement of this other one.	*Quisiera algunas copias de estas fotografías y ampliar esta otra.*	*Keesyayrah ahlgoonoass kopyahss day aystahs foatoagrahfeeahss ee ahmplyahr aystah oatrah.*

Vocabulary

glossy finish, matte	*acabado en brillo, mate*	*ahkahbahdhoa ayn breeyoa, mahtay*
enlargement	*ampliación*	*ahmplyahthyon*
camera	*cámara*	*kahmahrah*

spool	*carrete*	*kahrraytay*
copy	*copia*	*kopyah*
diaphragm	*diafragma*	*dyahfrahgmah*
slide	*diapositiva*	*dyahpoaseetieebhah*
trigger	*disparador*	*deespahrahdhoar*
exhibition	*exposición*	*aykspoaseethyon*
filter	*filtro*	*feeltroa*
flash	*flash*	*flahsh*
picture	*fotografía*	*foatoagrahfeeah*
wide lens	*gran angular*	*grahn ahngoolahr*
negative	*negativo*	*naygahteebhoa*
objective	*objetivo*	*oabkhayteebhoa*
film	*película*	*payleekoolah*
battery	*pila*	*peelah*
positive	*positivo*	*poseeteebhoa*
projector	*proyector*	*proyayktoar*
test	*prueba*	*prwaybah*
to develop	*revelar*	*raybhaylahr*
size	*tamaño*	*tahmahñoa*
zoom lens	*teleobjetivo*	*taylayoabkhayteebhoa*
tripod	*trípode*	*treepoaday*
finder	*visor*	*bheesoar*

3.4.2.3. Jewelry store, watchmaker´s shop

My watch gets behind, ahead, could you check it?	*Mi reloj se atrasa, adelanta, ¿podría revisarlo?*	*Mee rayloa say ahtrahsah, ahdhaylahntah, poadreeah raybheesahrloa?*
How much will it cost to fix it?	*¿Cuánto costará el arreglo?*	*Kwahntoa kostahrah ayl ahrraygloa?*
Could you change the writsband of the watch?	*¿Podría cambiarme la correa del reloj?*	*Poadreeah kambyahrmay lah koarrayah dayl rayloa?*
I would like a gold chain, how many karats is it?	*Desearía una cadenita de oro, ¿cuántos quilates tiene?*	*Daydayahreeah oonah kahdhayneetah day oaroa, kwahntoass keelahtayss tyaynay?*
Could I take a look at this necklace, watch, earrings, rings...?	*¿Podría ver ese collar, reloj, pendientes, anillo...?*	*Poadreeah bhayr aysay koyahr, rayloa, paydhyaytayss, aheeyoa....?*

Vocabulary

stainless steel	*acero inoxidable*	*ahthayroa eenoakseedhahblay*
aquamarine	*aguamarina*	*ahgwahmahreenah*
pin	*alfiler*	*ahlfeelayr*

amber	*ámbar*	*ahmbahr*
ring	*anillo*	*ahneeeyoa*
imitation jewelry	*bisutería*	*beesootayreeah*
bracelet	*brazalete*	*brahthahlaytay*
brilliant	*brillantes*	*breeyahntayss*
fastener	*broche*	*broachay*
chain	*cadena*	*kahdhaynah*
necklace	*collar*	*koyahr*
choral	*coral*	*korahl*
belt	*correa*	*korrayah*
chrome	*cromado*	*kroamahdhoa*
chronometer	*cronómetro*	*kroanoamaytroa*
cross	*cruz*	*krooth*
alarm clock	*despertador*	*dayspayrtahdhor*
diamond	*diamante*	*dyahmahntay*
gilding	*dorado*	*doarahdhoa*
lighter	*encendedor*	*ayncayndaydor*
emerald	*esmeralda*	*aysmayrahldhah*
twins	*gemelos*	*khaymayloass*
jewel	*joya*	*khoayah*
jeweler	*joyero*	*khoayayroa*
hand	*manecilla*	*mahnaytheeyah*
ivory	*marfil*	*mahrfeel*
locket	*medallón*	*Maydahyoan*
minute hand	*minutero*	*meenootayroa*
mount	*montura*	*moantoorah*
jetty	*muelle*	*mwayyay*

gold	oro	oaroa
earrings	pendientes	payndyaytayss
pearls	perlas	payrlahss
precious	piedra	pyaydrah
stone	preciosa	praythyoasah
silver	plata	plahtah
bracelet	pulsera	poolsayrah
karats	quilates	keelahtayss
clock	reloj	rayloa
ruby	rubí	roobee
second hand	segundero	saygoondayroa
turquoise	turquesa	toorkaysah
sapphire	zafiro	thahfeerao

3.4.2.4. Book store, stationary shop, kiosk

I would like a roadmap of...	Deseo un mapa de carreteras de...	Daysayoa oon mahpah day kahrraytayrahss day...
I would like a city map, do you have any books on the city?	Quisiera un plano de la ciudad, ¿tiene algún libro sobre la ciudad?	Keesyayrah oon plahnoa day lah thyoodhahdh, tyaynay ahlgoon leebroa soabray lah thoodhahdh?
Do you have a bilingual guide book in.... and ...?	¿Tiene alguna guía turística bilingüe, en... y...?	Tyaynay ahlgoonah geeah tooreesteekah beeleengway, ayn... ee...?

I would like a notebook with graph paper.	Desearía un cuaderno cuadriculado.	*Daysayahreeah oon kwahdaynoa kwahdreekoolahdhoa.*
Do you have gift wrap?	¿Tiene usted papel de regalo?	*Tyaynay oostayd pahpayl day raygahloa?*
I would like some stationery, envelopes and postcards of the city.	Quisiera papel de cartas y sobres y tarjetas postales de la ciudad.	*Keeyayrah pahpayl day kahrtahss ee soabrayss ee tahrkhaytahss poastahllayss day lah thyoodhahdh.*
Do you have any newspapers in... language?	¿Tiene prensa en el idioma…?	*Tyaynay praynsah ayn ayl eedyoamah…?*
I would like the last issue of... magazine?	Quisiera el último número de la revista...	*Keeyayrah ayl oolteemao noomayroa day lah raybheestah...*
How much is this comic?	¿Cuánto cuesta este tebeo?	*Kwahntoa kwaystah aystay taybayoa?*

City

Vocabulary

Bookshop	*Librería*	*Bookshop*
anthology	*antología*	*ahntoaloageeah*
atlas	*atlas*	*ahtlahss*
author	*autor*	*ahwtoar*

library	*biblioteca*	*beeblyoataykah*
biography	*biografía*	*byoagrahfeeah*
catalogue	*catálogo*	*kahtahloagoa*
science	*ciencia*	*thyaynthyah*
science-fiction	*ciencia-ficción*	*thyaynthyah-feekthyon*
collection	*colección*	*kolaykthyon*
comedy	*comedia*	*komaydyah*
cover	*cubierta*	*koobyaytah*
story	*cuento*	*kwayntoa*
dictionary	*diccionario*	*deekthyonahryoa*
edition	*edición*	*aydeethyon*
editorial	*editorial*	*aydeetoaryahl*
encyclopedia	*enciclopedia*	*ayntheekloapaydhyah*
essay	*ensayo*	*aynsayoa*
writer	*escritor*	*ayskreetoar*
grammar	*gramática*	*grahmahteekah*
tourist guide	*guía turística*	*geeah tooreesteekah*
index	*índice*	*endeethay*
bookseller	*librero*	*leebrayroa*
book	*libro*	*leebroa*
manual	*manual*	*mahnwahl*
road map	*mapa de carreteras*	*mahpah day kahrraytayrahss*
memories	*memorias*	*maymoaryahss*
novel	*novela*	*noabhaylah*
piece	*obra*	*oabrah*
city map	*plano de la ciudad*	*plahnoa day lah thyoodhahdh*

poem	*poema*	*poaymah*
poetry	*poesía*	*poayseeah*
publication	*publicación*	*poobleekahthyon*
title	*título*	*teetooloa*
translator	*traductor*	*trahdooktoar*
volume	*volumen*	*bhoaloomayn*
Stationery	*Papelería*	*Stationary*
calendar	*agenda*	*ahkhayndhah*
photo album	*álbum fotográfico*	*ahlboom foatoagrahfeekoa*
note pad	*bloc de notas*	*bloak day noatahss*
pen	*bolígrafo*	*boaleegrahfoa*
calendar	*calendario*	*kahlayndahryoa*
binder	*carpeta*	*kahrpaytah*
letters	*cartas*	*kahrtahss*
cardboard	*cartón*	*kahrtoan*
bristol board	*cartulina*	*kahrtooleenah*
compass	*compás*	*lompahss*
notebook	*cuaderno*	*kwahdaynoa*
thumbtack	*chincheta*	*cheenchaytah*
label	*etiqueta*	*ayteekaytah*
eraser	*goma de borrar*	*goamah day boarrahr*
sheet of paper	*hoja de papel*	*oakhah day pahpayl*
pencil	*lápiz*	*lahpeeth*
cards	*naipes*	*nahypayss*
paper	*papel*	*pahpayl*
paste	*pegamento*	*paygahmayntoa*

paintbrush	*pincel*	*Peenthayl*
postcard	*postal*	*poastahl*
calligraphy	*pluma*	*ploomah*
pen	*estilográfica*	*aysteeloagrahfeekah*
ruler	*regla*	*rayglah*
marker	*rotulador*	*roatoolahdoar*
sharpener	*sacapuntas*	*sahkahpoontahss*
envelope	*sobre*	*soabray*
ink	*tinta*	*teentah*
Kiosk	*Quiosco*	*Kiosk*
announcement	*anuncio*	*ahnoonthyoa*
article	*artículo*	*ahrteekoolao*
correspondent	*corresponsal*	*koarrayspoansahl*
chronicle	*crónica*	*kroaneekah*
issue	*fascículo*	*fahstheekooloa*
gazette	*gaceta*	*gahthaytah*
number	*número*	*noomayroa*
newspaper	*periódico*	*payryoadeekoa*
journalism	*periodismo*	*payryoadheesmoa*
journalist	*periodista*	*payryoadheestah*
press	*prensa*	*praynsah*
magazine	*revista*	*raybheestah*
subscription	*suscripción*	*sooskreepthyon*
supplement	*suplemento*	*sooplaymayntoa*
comic	*tebeo*	*taybayo*

3.4.2.5. Hairdresser´s, perfume shop

I would like to have a haircut, a shave.	*Deseo cortarme el pelo, afeitarme.*	*Daysayoa kortahrmay ayl payloa, ahfaytahrmay.*
I would like my hair cut very short, short, average, long.	*Quiero que me deje el pelo muy corto, corto, normal, largo.*	*Kyayroa kay may daykhay ayl payloa mwee kortoa, kortoa, noarmahl, lahrgoa.*
Part it on the right, left, center.	*La raya a la derecha, izquierda, centro.*	*Lah rahyah ah lah dayrahchah, eethkyaydhah, thaytroa.*
Wash my hair.	*¡Láveme la cabeza!*	*Yahbhaymay lah kahbaythah!*
I would like some aftershave.	*Quisiera una loción para después del afeitado.*	*Keeyayrah oonah loathyon pahrah daypwayss dayl ahfaytahdhoa.*
Will I have to wait long?	*¿Tendré que esperar mucho?*	*Tayndhray kay ayspayrahr moochoa?*
I would like a wash, trim and color.	*Deseo un lavado y marcado y teñirme el pelo.*	*Daysayoa oon lahbhahdhoa ee mahrcahdhoa ee tayñeermay ayl payloa.*

Please, don't use any hairspray.	*Por favor, no ponga laca.*	*Por fahbhor, noa poangah lahkah*
I want to change my hairstyle.	*Quisiera cambiar de peinado.*	*Keeyayrah kambyahr day paynahdhao*
How much do I owe you?	*¿Cuánto le debo?*	*Kwahntoa lay dayboa?*
I need a shampoo for oily hair, dry, normal.	*Déme un champú para cabellos grasos, secos, normales.*	*Daymay oon chahmpoo pahrah kahbayyoass grahsoass, saykoass, noarmahlayss.*
I would like a lotion and shaving cream.	*Quisiera una crema hidratante y un depilatorio.*	*Keeyayrah oonah kraymah eedhrahtahntay ee oon daypeelahtoaryoa.*
Could you give me ... perfume?	*¿Me podría dar un frasco de perfume marca...?*	*May podreeah dahr oon frahskoa day payrfoomay mahrkah...?*
I would like a deodorant.	*Desearía un desodorante.*	*daysayahreeah oon daysoadoarahntay.*

Vocabulary

Hairdresser's	Peluquería	*Hairdresser*
shaving	*afeitar*	*ahfaytahr*
beard	*barba*	*bahrbah*

mustache	*bigote*	*beegoatay*
brush	*brocha*	*broacha*
dandruff	*caspa*	*kahspah*
brush	*cepillo*	*thaypeeyoa*
color	*color*	*koloar*
cut	*corte*	*kortay*
cream	*crema*	*craymah*
shampoo	*champú*	*chahmpoo*
nailpolish	*esmalte de uñas*	*aysmahltay day ooñahss*
mirror	*espejo*	*ayspaykhoa*
bangs	*flequillo*	*flaykeeyoa*
friction	*fricción*	*freekthyon*
soap	*jabón*	*khahboan*
hairspray	*laca*	*lahkah*
wash	*lavado*	*lahbhahdhoa*
lotion	*loción*	*loathyon*
manicure	*manicura*	*mahneekoorah*
knife	*navaja*	*nahbhahkhah*
wavy	*ondulado*	*oandoolahdhoa*
sideburns	*patillas*	*pahteeyahss*
hairstyle	*peinado*	*paynahdhoa*
comb	*peine*	*paynay*
hair	*pelo*	*payloa*
wig	*peluca*	*paylookah*
barber, hairdresser	*peluquero*	*paylookayroa*
hairline	*raya*	*rayah*

frizz	*rizo*	reethoa
curls	*rulos*	rooloass
dryer	*secador*	saykahdoar
dry	*seco*	saykoa
colored	*teñido*	tayñeedhoa
scissors	*tijeras*	teekhayrahss
tint	*tinte*	teentay
towel	*toalla*	toahyah
braid	*trenza*	traynthah
Perfume shop	***Perfumería***	**Perfumes**
suntan oil	*aceite bronceador*	ahthaytay broanthayahdoar
cologne	*agua de colonia*	ahgwah day koaloanyah
toothbrush	*cepillo de dientes*	thaypeeyoa day dyaytayss
compresses	*compresas*	kompraysahss
fingernail clipper	*corta uñas*	kortah ooñahss
make-up	*cosméticos*	kosmayteekoass
creams	*cremas*	kraymahss
toothpaste	*dentífrico*	dayteefreekoa
deodorant	*desodorante*	daysoadoarahntay
sponge	*esponja*	ayspoankhah
shaving tissue	*hojas de afeitar*	oakhahss day ahfaytahr
lipstick	*lápiz de labios*	lahpeeth day lahbyoass

cleansing cream	leche limpiadora	laychay leempyahdoarah
make-up	maquillaje	mahkeeyahkhay
mascara	mascarilla	mahskahreeyah
knife tissue	pañuelos de papel	pahñwayloass day pahpayl
baby powder	polvos de talco	poalbhoass day tahlkoa
nail polish remover	quita esmaltes	keetah aysmahltayss
eyeliner	rímmel	reemmayl
eyeshadow	sombra	soambrah
vaporizer	vaporizador	bhahpoareethahdoar

3.4.2.6. Tobacco

I would like a packet of cigarrettes, tobacco for pipe.	Quisiera un paquete de cigarrillos, tabaco de pipa.	Keeyayrah oon pahkaytay daytheegahrreeyoass, tahbahkoa daypeepah.
Give me a box of matches, cigars.	Déme una caja de cerillas, de puros.	Daymay oonahkahkhah daythayreeyahss, daypooroass.
I would like a lighter.	Desearía un mechero.	Daysayreeah oonmaychayroa.
Do you have pipe tobacco?	¿Tiene tabaco de pipa?	Tyaynay tahbahkoaday peepah?

119

| Could you fill up this lighter with fluid? | ¿Podría cargarme este mechero de gas? | Podreeah kahgahrmay aystay maychayroa day gahss? |

Vocabulary

mouthpiece	boquilla	boakeeyah
cardboard of cigarettes	cartón de cigarrillos	kahrtoan day theegahrreeyoass
matches	cerillas	thayreeyahss
cigarettes	cigarrillos	theegahrreeyoas
lighter	encendedor	aynthayndaydoar
matches	fósforos	foasfoaroass
smoking	fumar	foomahr
gas	gas	gahss
gasoline	gasolina	gahsoaleenah
cigarette paper	papel de fumar	pahpayl day foomahr
pipe	pipa	peepah
butt	pitillera	peeteeyayrah
cigar	puro	pooroa
tobacco	tabaco	tahbahkoa

3.4.3. Department stores

| Where is the ladies' department, juniors, children's, men's? | ¿Dónde está la sección de señoras, jóvenes, niños, caballeros? | Doanday aystah lah saykthyon day sayñoarahss, khobhaynayss, neeñoass, kahbahyayroass? |

In what floor is the gift department?	¿En qué planta está la sección de artículos de regalos?	Ayn kay plahntah aystah lah saykthyon day ahrteekooloass day raygahloass?
Where is the ladder, the elevator, (lift)?	¿Por dónde está la escalera mecánica, el ascensor?	Por doanday aystah lah ayskahlayrah maycahneekah, ayl aythaynsoar?
I would like this gift wrapped, please take the pricetag off.	Quisiera que me lo empaquetara para regalo, quite el precio.	Keeyayrah kay may lo aympahkaytahrah pahrah raygahloa, keetay ayl praythyoa.
Where is the register? Check-off	¿Dónde está la caja?	Doanday aystah lah kahkhah?

City

Vocabulary

elevator, lift	ascensor	ahsthaynsoar
register	caja	kahkhah
ladder	escalera	ayskahlayrah
shelves	estantería	aystahntayreeah
counter	mostrador	moastrahdoar
package	paquete	pahkaytay
floor	piso	peesoa
first floor	planta baja	plahntah bahkhah
fitting room	probador	proabahdoar
section	sección	saykthyon

3.4.3.1. Clothing

I would like to try on this suit, these pants, this skirt...	*Quisiera probarme este traje, pantalón, esta falda...*	*keeyayrah proabahrmay aystay trahkhay, pahntahloan, aystha fahldhah...*
Could I try it on?	*¿Puedo probármelo?*	*Pwaydoa proabahrmayloa?*
I like this one, although it's narrow, wide, big, tight.	*Éste me gusta, aunque me está estrecho, ancho, grande, justo.*	*Aystay may goostah, ahnoonkay may aystah aystraychoa, ahnchoa, grahnday, khoostoa.*
Do you have a bigger, smaller size?	*¿Tiene una talla mayor, menor?*	*Tyaynay oonah tahyah mahyoar, maynoar.?*
Do you have this skirt in a lighter, darker color?	*¿Tiene esta falda en un tono más claro, oscuro?*	*Tyaynay aystah fahldhah ayn oon toanoa mahss klahroa, oaskooroa?*
My size is...	*Mi talla es...*	*Mee tahyah ayss....*
Could you take my measurements?	*¿Puede tomarme la medida?*	*Pwayday toamahrmay lah maydheedhah?*
Could you do some alterations?	*¿Puede arreglarlo?*	*Pwayday ahrrayglahrloa?*

How many days will it take?	*¿Cuántos días tardará?*	*Kwahntoass deeahss tahrdhahrah?*
I need it by..	*Lo necesito para...*	*Loa naythayseetoa pahrah...*
Could you show me that print fabric?	*¿Puede enseñarme aquella tela estampada?*	*Pwayday aynsaypñahrmay ahkayyah taylah aystahmpahdhah?*
Is it cotton, wool...?	*¿Es de algodón, lana...?*	*Ayss day ahlgoadoan, lahnah...?*
Where are the fitting rooms?	*¿Dónde está el probador?*	*Doanday aystah ayl porabahdoar?*

Vocabulary

Garments	*Prendas*	*Prendas*
coat	*abrigo*	*ahbreegoa*
jacket	*americana*	*ahmayreekahnah*
swimsuit	*bañador*	*bahñahdoar*
robe	*bata*	*bahtah*
blouse	*blusa*	*bloosah*
button	*botón*	*boatoan*
panties	*bragas*	*brahgahss*
fastener	*broche*	*broachay*
scarf	*bufanda*	*boofahndhah*
socks	*calcetines*	*kahlthayteenayss*
underpants	*calzoncillos*	*kahlthoantheeyoass*
shirt	*camisa*	*kahmeesah*

undershirt	camiseta	Kahmeesaytah
hunting shirt	cazadora	kahthahdhoarah
belt	cinturón	theentooroan
ensemble	combinación	kombeenahthyon
tie	corbata	korbahtah
zipper	cremallera	kraymahyayrah
vest	chaleco	chahlaykoa
jacket	chaqueta	chahkaytah
slip	enagua	aynahgwah
girdle	faja	fahkhah
skirt	falda	fahldhah
gaberdine	gabardina	gahbahrdeenah
gloves	guantes	gwahntayss
raincoat	impermeable	eempayrmayahblay
sweater	jersey	khayrsay
stockings	medias	maydyahss
pants	pantalones	pahntahloanayss
handkerchifs	pañuelos	pahñwayloass
underwear	ropa interior	roapah eentayryoar
hat	sombrero	soambrayroa
brazier	sostén	soastayn
bra	sujetador	sookhaytahdoar
dress	vestido	bhayteedhoa
shoes	zapatos	thahpahtoass
Fabrics	*Tejidos*	*Fabrics*
acrylic	acrílico	ahkreeleekoa
cotton	algodón	ahlgoadoan
buckskin	ante	ahntay
leather	cuero	kwayroa
lace	encaje	aynkahkhay
knitted	de punto	day poontoa

felt	*fieltro*	*fyayltroa*
flannel	*franela*	*frahnaylah*
gauze	*gasa*	*gahsah*
thread	*hilo*	*eeloa*
wool	*lana*	*lahnah*
nylon	*nailon*	*nahyloan*
corduroy	*pana*	*pahnah*
satin	*raso*	*rahsoa*
silk	*seda*	*saydah*
velvet	*terciopelo*	*tayrthyoapayloa*

3.4.3.2. Shoes

I would like a ... pair of shoes, made of leather, with a leather sole, rubber.	*Quiero un par de zapatos de color..., de piel, con suela de cuero, goma.*	*kyayroa oon pahr day thahpahtoass day koloar...., day pyayl, kon swaylah day kwayroa, goamah.*
What size do you wear?	*¿Qué número calza?*	*Kay noomayroa kahlthah?*
My size is forty one.	*Mi número es el 41.*	*Mee noomayroa ayss ayl (41) cwahrayntah ee oonoa*
When can I pick them up?	*¿Cuándo puedo venir a recogerlos?*	*Kwahndoa pwaydoa bhayneer ah raykoakhayrloass?*
Could you give me half-soles?	*¿Me puede poner medias suelas?*	*May pwayday poanayr aydyahss swaylahss?*

They are a little small, narrow, wide, somewhat big.	*Me quedan un poco pequeños, estrechos, anchos, algo grandes.*	*May kaydhahn oon poakoa paykayñoas, aystraychoass, ahnchoass, ahlgoa grahndayss*
Do you have a larger, smaller size of this same shoe?	*¿Tiene un número mayor, menor de este mismo modelo?*	*Tyaynay oon noomayroa mahyoar, maynoar day aystay meesmoa moadayloa?*
Would you have this same shoe in another color?	*¿Tendría este mismo modelo en otro color?*	*Tayndreeah aystay meesmoa moadayloa ayn oatroa koloar?*
Could you show me those boots, the ones on the window?	*¿Puede enseñarme aquellas botas que hay en el escaparate?*	*Pwayday aynsayñahrmay ahkayyahss boatahss kay ahy ayn ayl ayskahpahrahtay?*
Could you fix the heel of this shoe?	*¿Me puede arreglar el tacón del zapato?*	*May pwayday ahrrayglahr ayl tahkon dayl thahpahtoa?*
I need a little polish, brown shoestrings, black.	*Necesitaría un poco de betún, unos cordones marrones, negros.*	*Naythayseetahreeah oon poakoa day baytoon, oonoass kordoanayss mahrroanayss, naygroass*

Vocabulary

polish	*betún*	Baytoon
boots	*botas*	boatahss
shoehorn	*calzador*	kahlthahdoar
cord	*cordón*	kordoan
leather	*cuero*	kwayroa
rubber	*goma*	goamah
buckle	*hebilla*	aybeeyah
tongue	*lengüeta*	layngwaytah
measure	*medida*	maydheedhah
foot	*pie*	pyay
insole	*plantilla*	plahnteeyah
sandal	*sandalia*	sahndhahlyah
sole	*suela*	swaylah
heel	*tacón*	tahkon
slipper	*zapatilla*	thahpahteeyah
shoe	*zapato*	thahpahtoa

3.5. Leisure, tourist sights and sports

3.5.1. Tourist sights

| Where is the tourist office? | *¿Dónde está la oficina de turismo?* | Doanday aystah lah oafeetheenah day tooreesmoa? |
| What are the most important artistic monuments of this city? | *¿Cuáles son los monumentos artísticos más importantes de la ciudad?* | Kwahlayss soan loass moanoomayntoass ahrteesteekoass mahss eempoartahntayss day lah hyoodhahdh? |

Do you have a city map, of the sorrounding areas?	¿Tiene un plano de la ciudad, de los alrededores?	*Tyaynay oon plahnoa day lah thyoodhahdh, day loass ahlraydhaydhoarays?*
Is there an organized tour to visit the old city?	¿Existe alguna ruta turística organizada para visitar la ciudad antigua?	*Aykseetay ahlgoonah rootah tooreesteekah oargahneethahdhah pahrah bheeseetahr lah thyoodhahdh ahnteegwah?*
How much is the excursion?	¿Cuánto cuesta la excursión?	*Kwahnto kwaystah lah aykskoorthyon?*
When does it start and when does it finish?	¿A qué hora empieza y a qué hora acaba?	*Ah kay oarah aympyaythah ee ah kay oarah ahkahbah?*
Where is the Parliament, the cathedral, the church of...?	¿Dónde está el Parlamento, la catedral, la iglesia de...?	*Doanday aystah ayl Pahrlahmayntoa, lah kahtaydrahl, lah eeglaysyah day...?*
What is this church called?	¿Cómo se llama esta iglesia?	*Koamoa say yahmah aystaheeglaysyah?*
I would like to visit... How much time does it take to walk there?	Desearía visitar... ¿Cuánto tiempo se tarda andando?	*Daysayahreeah bheeseetahr... Kwahnto tyaympao say tahrdhah ahndhahndhoa?*

English	Spanish	Pronunciation
What period and style does it belong to?	¿De qué época es y de qué estilo?	*Day kay aypoakah ayss ee day kay aysteeloa?*
What artistic movement is it?	¿De qué estilo artístico es?	*Day kay aysteeloa ahrteesteekoa ayss?*
Can one climb the tower?	¿Es posible subir a la torre?	*Ayss poaseeblay soobeer ah lah toarray?*

Vocabulary

English	Spanish	Pronunciation
abbey	*abadía*	*ahbahdyeeah*
apse	*ábside*	*ahbseeday*
sidewalk	*acera*	*ahthayrah*
aquarium	*acuario*	*ahkooahryoa*
agency	*agencia*	*ahkhaynthyah*
surroundings	*alrededores*	*ahlraydaydoarayss*
old	*antiguo*	*ahnteegwoa*
file	*archivo*	*ahrcheebhoa*
architecture	*arquitectura*	*ahkeetayktoorah*
art	*arte*	*ahrtay*
craft	*artesanía*	*ahrtaysahneeah*
avenue	*avenida*	*ahbhayneedhah*
city council	*ayuntamiento*	*ahyoontahmyayntoa*
bath	*balneario*	*bahlnayahryoa*
bank	*banco*	*bahnkoa*
district	*barrio*	*bahrryoa*
basilica	*basílica*	*bahseeleekah*

garbage	basura	bahsoorah
bag	bolsa	boalsah
vault	bóveda	boabhaydhah
street	calle	kahyay
steeple	campanario	kahmpahmahryoa
chapel	capilla	kahpeeyah
capital	capital	kahpeetahl
capitel	capitel	kapeetayl
castle	castillo	kahsteeyoa
cathedral	catedral	kahtaydrahl
cementery	cementerio	thaymayntayryoa
center	centro	thaytroa
cinema	cine	theenay
city	ciudad	thyoodhahdh
civilization	civilización	theebheeleethahthyon
cloister	claustro	klahwstroa
column	columna	koloomnah
construction	construcción	konstrookthyon
contamination	contaminación	kontahmeenahthyon
convent	convento	konbhayntoa
barracks	cuartel	kwahrtayl
dome	cúpula	koopoolah
decoration	decorado	daykorahdhoa
building	edificio	aydeefeethyoa
era	época	aypoakah
window	escaparate	ayskahpahrahtay
school	escuela	ayskwaylah

sculpture	*escultura*	*Ayskooltoorah*
corner	*esquina*	*aykeenah*
establishment	*establecimiento*	*aystahblaytheemyayntoa*
stadium	*estadio*	*aystahdyoa*
statue	*estatua*	*aystahtwah*
style	*estilo*	*aysteeloa*
exhibition	*exposición*	*ayksoaseethyon*
factory	*fábrica*	*fahbreekah*
façade	*fachada*	*fahchahdhah*
fair	*feria*	*fayryah*
fortress	*fortaleza*	*foarttahlaythah*
mural	*fresco*	*frayskoa*
fountain	*fuente*	*fwayntay*
art gallery	*galería de arte*	*gahlayreeah day ahrtay*
hospital	*hospital*	*oaspeetahl*
church	*iglesia*	*eeglayseeah*
garden	*jardín*	*khahdheen*
lake	*lago*	*lahgoa*
tablet	*lápida*	*lahpeedhah*
market	*mercado*	*mayrkahdhoa*
monastery	*monasterio*	*moanahstayryoa*
monument	*monumento*	*moanoonayntoa*
mosaic	*mosaico*	*moasahykoa*
walls	*murallas*	*moorahyahss*
museum	*museo*	*moosayoa*
nave	*nave*	*nahbhay*
pavilion	*pabellón*	*pahbayyoan*

City

landscape	paisaje	Pahysahkhay
palace	palacio	pahlahthyoa
wastepaper basket	papelera	pahpaylayrah pahrayd
wall	pared	pahrkay
park	parque	pahrteedhoa
game	partido	pahtyoa
patio	patio	peentoar
painter	pintor	peentoorah
painting	pintura	peestheenah
pool	piscina	plahnoa day lah
city map	plano de la ciudad	thyoodhahdh
square	plaza	plahthah
portico	pórtico	poartekoa
bridge	puente	pwayntay
residence	residencia	raydeedaynthyah
river	río	reeoa
rose window	rosetón	roasaytoan
ruins	ruinas	rweeanahss
arcades	soportales	soapoartahlayss
theater	teatro	tayahtroa
terrace	terraza	tayrrahthah
stain glass window	vidriera	bheedhryayrah
window	vista	bheestah
panoramic view	panorámica	pahnoarahm
zoo	zoológico	thooaloakheekoa

3.5.1.2. Museums

Where is the... museum?	¿Dónde está el museo de...?	Doanday aystah ayl moosayoa day...?
How much are the tickets to this museum, exposition...?	¿Cuánto cuesta la entrada a este museo, esta exposición...?	kwahntoa kwaystah lah ayntrahdhah ah aystay moosayoa, aystah aykspoaseethyon...?
When does it close?	¿A qué hora cierran?	Ah kay oarah thyayrrahn?
Can you take pictures?	¿Se pueden hacer fotografías?	Say pwaydayn ahthayr foatoagrahfeeahss?
Are there guided visits?	¿Hay guía para visitas?	Ahy geeah pahrah bheeseetahss?
I would like to buy a catalogue.	Desearía comprar el catálogo.	Daysayahreeah komprahr ayl kahtahloagoa.
How long will this exhibition be here?	¿Hasta cuándo estará aquí la exposición?	Ahstah kwahndoa aystahrah ahkee lah aykspoaseethyon?

City

Vocabulary

old	antiguo	ahnteegwoa
armor	armadura	ahrmahdoorah

artist	artista	ahrteestah
low relief	bajo relieve	bahkhoa raylyaybhay
still life	bodegón	boadaygoan
bust	busto	boostao
catalogue	catálogo	kahtahloagoa
ceramic	cerámica	thayrahmeekah
collection	colección	kolaykthyon
painting	cuadro	kwahdroa
drawing	dibujo	deebookhoa
entrance	entrada	ayntrahdhah
time	época	aypoakah
sculptor	escultor	ayskooltoar
sculpture	escultura	ayskooltoorah
prints	estampa	aystahmahpah
statue	estatua	aystahtwah
style	estilo	aysteeloa
excavations	excavaciones	aykskahbhahthyonss
exhibition	exposición	aykspoaseethyon
foundation	fundación	foondahthyon
engraving	grabado	grahbahdhoa
canvas	lienzo	lyaynthoa
lithograph	litografía	leetoagrahfeeah
manuscript	manuscrito	mahnooskreetoa
miniature	miniatura	meenyahtoorah
coin	moneda	moanaydhah
mummy	momia	moamyah
mosaic	mosaico	mosahykoa

museum	*museo*	*Moosayoa*
landscape	*paisaje*	*pahysahkhay*
art gallery	*pinacoteca*	*peenahkotaykah*
project	*proyecto*	*proayayktoa*
realism	*realismo*	*rayahleesmoa*
reconstruction	*reconstrucción*	*raykonstrookthyon*
relief	*relieve*	*raylyaybhay*
reproduction	*reproducción*	*rayprodookthyon*
restoration	*restauración*	*raystahwrahthyon*
altarpiece	*retablo*	*raytahbloa*
portrait	*retrato*	*raytrahtoa*
ruins	*ruinas*	*rweenahss*
room	*sala*	*sahlah*
century	*siglo*	*seegloa*
tapestry	*tapiz*	*tahpeeth*
visit	*visita*	*bheeseetah*
visitors	*visitantes*	*bheeseetahntay*
Art	*Arte*	*Art*
abstract	*abstracto*	*ahbstrahktoa*
arabic	*árabe*	*ahrahbay*
baroque	*barroco*	*bahrroakoa*
contemporary	*contemporáneo*	*kontaympoarahnayoa*
cubist	*cubista*	*koobeestah*
expressionist	*expresionista*	*aykspraythyoneestah*
gothic	*gótico*	*goateekoa*
greek	*griego*	*greeyagoa*
impressionist	*impresionista*	*lyaynthoa*

City

modern	*moderno*	*moadayrnoa*
neoclassicist	*neoclásico*	*nayoaklahseekoa*
realist	*realista*	*rayahleestah*
renaissance	*renacentista*	*raynahthaynteestah*
romanic	*románico*	*roamahneekoa*

3.5.1.3. Theater and cinema

Are there any tickets available for tonight's show?	*¿Quedan localidades para la función de esta noche?*	*Kaydhahn loakahleedhahdha yss pahrah lah foonthyon day aystah noachay?*
What is playing at the cinema, showing at the theatre this afternoon, tonight?	*¿Qué ponen en el cine, teatro esta tarde, noche?*	*Kay poanayn ayn ayl theenay, tayahtroa aystah tahrday, noachay?*
Is the film dubbed?	*¿La película está doblada?*	*Lah payleekoolah aystah doablahdhah?*
When does the play start?	*¿A qué hora empieza la obra?*	*Ah kay oarah aympyaythah lah oabrah?*
Where can you get tickets?	*¿Dónde se pueden adquirir las localidades?*	*Doanday say pwaydhah ahdhkeereer lahss loakahleedhahdha yss?*

City

I would like to reserve some tickets for...	*Desearía reservar localidades para...*	*Daysayahreeah raysayrbhahr loakahleedhahdha yss pahrah...*
Could I have a program, please?	*¿Me da un programa, por favor?*	*May dah oon proagrahmah, por fahbhor?*
What is the program for tonight's concert?	*¿Cuál es el programa del concierto de esta tarde?*	*Kwahl ayss ayl proagrahmah dayl konthyayrtoa day aystah tahrday?*
I would like to reserve two seats in the balcony.	*Quisiera reservar dos localidades en el patio de butacas.*	*Keesyayrah raysayrbhahr doss loakaleedhahdhayss ayn ayl pahtyoa day bootahkahss*
I'm sorry, it's sold out.	*Lo siento, las localidades están agotadas.*	*Loa syayntoa, lahss loakaleedhahdhayss aystahn ahgoatahdhahss.*

Vocabulary

Theater and cinema	*Teatro y cine*	Theater and cinema
usher	*acomodador*	*ahkomoadhahdhoar*
act	*acto*	*ahktoa*
actor	*actor*	*ahktoar*
actress	*actriz*	*ahktreeth*
acoustics	*acústica*	*ahkoosteekah*
applause	*aplausos*	*ahplahwsoass*

City

137

seat	*asiento*	*ahsyayntoa*
soundtrack	*banda de sonido*	*bahndhah day soaneedhoa*
wings	*bastidores*	*bahsteedhoarayss*
ticket	*billete*	*beeyaytay*
dressing room	*camerino*	*kahmayreenoa*
poster	*cartel*	*kahrtayl*
cinema	*cine*	*theenay*
circus	*circo*	*theerkoa*
queue	*cola*	*kolah*
comedy	*comedia*	*komaydyah*
procession	*comparsa*	*kompahrah*
short film	*cortometraje*	*kortoamaytrahkhay*
animated cartoons	*dibujos animados*	*deebookhoass ahneemahdhoass*
direction	*dirección*	*deeraykthyon*
director	*director*	*deerayktoar*
dubbing	*doblaje*	*doablahkhay*
documentary	*documental*	*dokoomayntahl*
drama	*drama*	*drahmah*
entrance	*entrada*	*ayntrahdha*
scene	*escena*	*aysthaynah*
stage	*escenario*	*aysthaynahryoa*
set	*escenografía*	*aysthaynoagrahfeeah*
show	*espectáculo*	*ayspayktahkooloa*
spectator	*espectador*	*aypayktahdoar*
premiere	*estreno*	*aystraynoa*
festival	*festival*	*faysteebhahl*
line	*fila*	*feelah*
end	*fin*	*feen*

English	Spanish	Pronunciation
gallery	*galería*	*gahlayreeah*
twins	*gemelos*	*khaymayloass*
wardrobes	*guardarropas*	*gwahrdahrroapahss*
script	*guión*	*gweeoan*
interval	*intermedio*	*eentayrmaydyoa*
interpretation	*interpretación*	*eentayrpraytahthyon*
film	*largometraje*	*lahrgoamaytrahkhay*
setting	*localidad*	*loakahleedhahdh*
marionettes	*marionetas*	*mahryoanaytahss*
editing	*montaje*	*moantahkhay*
play	*obra*	*oabrah*
opera	*ópera*	*oapayrah*
box	*palco*	*pahlkoa*
screen	*pantalla*	*pahntahyah*
balcony	*patio de butacas*	*pahtyoa day bootahkahss*
movie	*película*	*payleekoolah*
character	*personaje*	*payrsoanahkhay*
hooters	*pitos*	*peetoass*
program	*programa*	*prograhmah*
protagonist	*protagonista*	*protahgoaneestah*
projection	*proyección*	*proyaykthyon*
projector	*proyector*	*proyayktoar*
public	*público*	*poobleekoa*
recital	*recital*	*raytheetahl'*
representation	*representación*	*raypraysayntahthyon*
reservation	*reserva*	*raysayrbhah*
exit	*salida*	*sahleedhah*
box office	*taquilla*	*tahkeeyah*
theater	*teatro*	*tayahtroa*

curtain	*telón*	*tayloan*
season	*temporada*	*taympoarahdhah*
text	*texto*	*taykstoa*
time	*tiempo*	*tyaympoa*
puppets	*títeres*	*teetayrayss*
title	*título*	*teetooloa*
tragedy	*tragedia*	*trahkhaydyah*
plot	*trama*	*trahmah*
lobby	*vestíbulo*	*bhaysteebooloa*
wardrobe	*vestuario*	*bhaystwahryoa*
voice	*voz*	*bhoth*
operetta	*zarzuela*	*thahrthwaylah*
Opera, concerts, ballet	***Ópera, conciertos, ballet***	*Opera, concerts, ballet*
aria	*aria*	*ahryah*
dancer	*bailarín*	*bahylahreen*
ballerina	*bailarina*	*bahylahreenah*
dance	*baile*	*bahylay*
ballet	*ballet*	*bahyayt*
band	*banda*	*bahndhah*
baton	*batuta*	*bahtootah*
bolero	*bolero*	*boalayroa*
song	*canto*	*kahntoa*
composition	*composición*	*kompoaseethyon*
composer	*compositor*	*komposeetoar*
concert	*concierto*	*konthyayrtoa*
choreography	*coreografía*	*korayoagrahfeeah*
choir	*coro*	*koroa*
quartet	*cuarteto*	*kwahrtaytoa*

dance	danza	dhahnthah
duet	dúo	dhooa
show	espectáculo	ayspayktahkooloa
study	estudio	aystoodyoa
phillarmonic	filarmónica	feelahrmoaneekah
group	grupo	groopoa
interpreter	intérprete	eentayrpraytay
overture	obertura	oabayrtoorah
orchestra	orquesta	oarkaystah
score	partitura	pahrteetoorah
quintet	quinteto	keentaytoa
concert hall	sala de conciertos	sahlah day konthyayrtoass
symphony	sinfonía	seenfoaneeah
soloist	solista	soaleestah
sonata	sonata	soanahtah
sound	sonido	soaneedhoa
trio	trío	treeoa
waltz	vals	bhahlss
Singers	*Cantantes*	**Singers**
bass	bajo	bahkhoa
baritone	barítono	bahreetoanoa
contralto	contralto	kontrahltoa
mezzo soprano	medio soprano	maydyoa soaprahnoa
soprano	soprano	soaprahnoa
tenor	tenor	taynoar
Music	*Música*	**Music**
old	antigua	ahnteegwah
classical	clásica	kaahseekah
contemporary	contemporánea	kontaympoarahnayah

chamber	de cámara	day kahmahrah
jazz	jazz	jahth
modern	moderna	moadayrnah
pop	pop	poap
rock	rock	roak
sacred	sacra	sahkrah
symphonic	sinfónica	seenfoaneekah
Instruments	*Instrumentos*	*Instruments*
accordion	acordeón	ahkoardayoan
harp	arpa	ahrpah
battery	batería	bahtayreeah
clarinet	clarinete	klahreenaytay
contrabass	contrabajo	kontahbahkhoa
bassoon	fagot	fahgoat
flute	flauta	flahwtah
guitar	guitarra	geetahrrah
mandolin	mandolina	mahndoaleenah
oboe	oboe	oaboay
piano	piano	pyahnoa
cymbals	platillos	plahteeyoass
saxophone	saxofón	sahksoafoan
drum	tambor	tahmboar
kettledrum	tímpano	teempahnoa
trombone	trombón	troamboan
trumpet	trompeta	troampaytah
viola	viola	bhyoalah
violin	violín	bhyoaleen
violenccelo	violonchelo	bhyoaloanchayloa

Club	Discoteca	Clubs
partner	*acompañante*	*ahkompahñahntay*
dancing	*bailar*	*bahylahr*
counter	*barra*	*bahrrah*
drink	*bebida*	*baybeedhah*
toast	*brindis*	*breendheess*
waiter	*camarero*	*kahmahrayroa*
singer	*cantante*	*kahntahntay*
musical group	*conjunto musical*	*konkhoontoa mooseekahl*
consumption	*consumición*	*konsoomeethyon*
entrance	*entrada*	*ayntrahdhah*
show	*espectáculo*	*ayspayktahkooloa*
table	*mesa*	*maysah*
reservation	*reserva*	*raysayrbhah*
party hall	*sala de fiestas*	*sahlah day fyaystahss*
charts	*tablas*	*tahblahss*

3.5.1.4. Sports

Could you tell me if there is a football game today, basketball, tennis?	*¿Me podría decir si hoy hay algún partido de fútbol, baloncesto, tenis?*	*May podreeah daytheer see oi ahy ahlgoon pahrteedhoa day footboal, bahloanthaystoa, taynees?*
What teams are playing?	*¿Qué equipos juegan?*	*Kay aykeepoass khwaygahn?*
Where is the football field?	*¿Dónde está el campo de fútbol?*	*Doanday aystah ayl kahmpoa day fooboal?*

City

143

When does the game start?	¿A qué hora empieza el encuentro?	Ah kay oarah aympyaythah ayl aynkwayntroa?
How much is the ticket for the event, the race, the game?	¿Qué vale la entrada para el acontecimiento, la carrera, el encuentro?	Kay bhahlay lah ayntrahdhah pahrah ayl ahkontaytheemyayntoa, lah kahrrayrah, ayl aynkwayntroa?
Is there a pool or club around here?	¿Hay alguna piscina o club por esta zona?	Ahy ahlgoonah peeseenah oa kloob por aystah thoanah?
Can one swim in this river, lake?	¿Se puede bañar uno en este río, lago?	Say pwayday bahñahr oonoa ayn aystay reeoa, lahgoa?
Could you tell me where the car races, motorcycle, bycicle are held?	¿Podría decirme dónde se celebran las carreras de coches, motos, ciclistas?	Podreeah daytheermay doanday say thaylaybrahn lahss kahrrayrahss. day koachayss, moatoass, theekleestahss?
Where is the horse track?	¿Dónde está el hipódromo?	Doanday aystah ayl eepoadroamoa?
Where can you place bets, in the horse track?	¿En qué zona del hipódromo se pueden realizar las apuestas?	Ayn kay thoanah dayl eepoadroamoa say pwaydayn rayahleethahr lahss ahpwaystahss?

I would like to ride a bycicle.	*Desearía pasear en bicicleta.*	*Daysayahreeah pahsayahr ayn beetheeklaytah.*

Vocabulary

fan	*aficionado*	*ahfeethyonahdhoa*
referee	*árbitro*	*ahrbeetroa*
athlete	*atleta*	*ahtlaytah*
boat	*barca*	*bahrkah*
bicycle	*bicicleta*	*beetheeklaytah*
stables	*caballerizas*	*kahbahyayreethahss*
champion	*campeón*	*kahmpayoan*
football field	*campo de fútbol*	*Kahmpoa day footboal*
fishing rod	*caña de pescar*	*kahñah day payskahr*
race	*carrera*	*kahrrayrah*
hunt	*caza*	*kahthah*
hunter	*cazador*	*kahthahdhoar*
classification	*clasificación*	*klahseefeekahthyon*
competition	*competición*	*kompayteethyon*
runner	*corredor*	*korraydhoar*
summit	*cumbre*	*koombray*
sport	*deporte*	*daypoartay*
disqualifying	*descalificar*	*dayskahleefeekahr*
untie	*desempate*	*daysaympahtay*
sport discipline	*disciplina deportiva*	*deestheepleenah daypoarteebhah*
craft	*embarcación*	*aymbahrkahthyon*
tiing	*empatar*	*aympahtahr*

tie, draw	empate	aympahtay
trainer	entrenador	ayntraynahdoar
training	entrenamiento	ayntraynahmyayntoa
team	equipo	aykeepoa
escalade	escalada	ayskahlahdhah
shotgun	escopeta	ayskopaytah
skis	esquís	aykeess
stadium	estadio	aystahdyoa
trip	excursión	aykskoorthyon
finalist	finalista	feenahleestah
footballer	futbolista	footboaleestah
gym	gimnasio	kheemnahsyoa
race track	hipódromo	eepoadroamoa
player	jugador	khoogahdoar
fishing license	licencia de pesca	leethaynthyah day payskah
marathon	maratón	mahrahtoan
medal	medalla	maydahyah
goal	meta	maytah
olympics	olimpiada	oaleempyahdhah
game	partido	pahrteedhoa
skates	patines	pahteenayss
ball	pelota	payloatah
lose	perder	payrdayr
fishing	pesca	payskah
pool	piscina	peestheenah
track	pista	peestah
tennis court	pista de tenis	peestah day tayneess
goal	portería	poartayreeah
goal keeper	portero	poartayroa

test	*prueba*	*Prwaybah*
racket	*raqueta*	*rahkaytah*
record	*récord*	*raykoardh*
net	*red*	*raydh*
rowing	*remar*	*raymahr*
oar	*remo*	*raymoa*
jump	*salto*	*sahltoa*
time	*tiempo*	*tyaympoa*
helm	*timón*	*teemoan*
track field	*velódromo*	*bhayloadroamoa*
wardrobe	*vestuario*	*bhaystwahyoa*

Deportes	Deportes	*Sports*
mountaineering	*alpinismo*	*ahlpeeneesmoa*
athletics	*atletismo*	*ahtlayeesmoa*
basketball	*baloncesto*	*bahloanthaystao*
handball	*balonmano*	*bahloanmahnoa*
volleyball	*balonvolea*	*bahloanbhoalayah*
baseball	*béisbol*	*baysboal*
boxing	*boxeo*	*boaksayoa*
races	*carreras*	*kahrrarahss*
hunting	*caza*	*kahthah*
cycling	*ciclismo*	*theekleesmoa*
horsemanship	*equitación*	*aykeetahthyon*
fencing	*esgrima*	*aysgreemah*
ski	*esquí*	*ayskee*
football	*fútbol*	*footboal*
gymnastics	*gimnasia*	*kheemnahsyah*
golf	*golf*	*goalf*
weight lifting	*halterofilia*	*ahltayroafeelyah*
hockey	*hockey*	*oakay*

judo	*judo*	khoodhoa
karate	*kárate*	kahrhatay
discus throwing	*lanzamiento de disco*	lahnthahmyayntoa day deeskoa
free fight	*lucha libre*	loochah leebray
motorcycling	*motorismo*	moatoareesmoa
swimming	*natación*	nahtahthyon
skating	*patinaje*	pahteenahkhay
fishing	*pesca*	payskah
ping-pong	*ping-pong*	peeng-poang
polo	*polo*	poaloa
rowing	*remo*	raymoa
rugby	*rugby*	roogby
tennis	*tenis*	taynees

3.5.1.5. Beach, mountains and the countryside

Could you tell me where I can find a quiet beach?	*¿Podría indicarme una playa tranquila?*	Podreeah eendeekahrmay oonah plahyah trahnkeelah?
Where can I rent a beach umbrella and a lawn chair, please?	*¿Dónde puedo alquilar una sombrilla y unas tumbonas, por favor?*	Doanday pwaydhoa ahlkeelahr oonah soambreeyah ee oonahss toomboanahss, por fahbhor?
Is it safe to swim in this beach?	*¿Se puede nadar sin peligro en esta playa?*	Say pwaydhay nahdhahr seen payleegroa ayn aystah plahyah?

Where can I rent a boat?	¿Dónde puedo alquilar una embarcación?	Doanday pwaydhoa ahlkeelahr oonah aymbahrkahthyon?
Are there any dangerous currents?	¿Hay alguna corriente peligrosa?	Igh ahlgoonah korryayntay payleegroasah?
The water is cold, hot, clean, dirty, muddy.	El agua está fría, caliente, limpia, sucia, turbia.	Ayl ahgwah aystah freeah, kahlyayntah, leempyah, soothyah, toorbyah.
Is the nearest town very far?	¿Está muy lejos el pueblo más cercano?	Aystah mwee laykhoass ayl pwaybloa mahss thayrkahnoa?
We would like to take an excursion around the mountains, do you have a map of the roads, inns, trails?	Deseamos hacer una excursión por la montaña, ¿tendría algún mapa de los caminos, albergues, senderos?	Daysayahmoass ahthayr oonah aykskoorsyon por lah moantahñah, Tayndreeah ahlgoon mahpah day loass kahmeenoass, ahlbayrgayss, sayndayroass?
Do these mountains have refuges where one can spend the night?	¿Estas montañas tienen refugios donde poder pasar la noche?	Aystahss moantahñahss tyaynayn rayfookhyoass doanday podhayr pahsahr lah noachay?

| I would like to rent mountainiering equipment, ski equipment. | *Quisiera alquilar un equipo de montaña, esquí...* | *Keesyayrah ahlkeelahr oon aykeepoa day moantahñah, ayskee...* |
| Is there a typical celebration in the towns of this area? | *¿Hay alguna fiesta típica en los pueblos de la zona?* | *Ighahlgoonah fyaystah teepeekah ayn loass pwaybloass day lah thoanah?* |

Vocabulary

camped	*acampada*	*akahmpahdhah*
drinkable water	*agua potable*	*ahgwah poatahblay*
air	*aire*	*ahyray*
fins	*aletas*	*ahlaytahss*
algae	*algas*	*ahlgahss*
animal	*animal*	*ahneemahl*
tree	*árbol*	*ahrboal*
sand	*arena*	*ahraynah*
stream	*arroyo*	*ahrroayoa*
bay	*bahía*	*baheeah*
bath	*balneario*	*bahlnayahryoa*
bath	*baño*	*bahñoa*
boat	*barca*	*bahrkah*
cane	*bastón*	*bahstoan*
forest	*bosque*	*boaskay*
boots	*botas*	*boatahss*
suntan	*bronceado*	*broanthayahdhoa*
dive	*buceo*	*boothayoa*

road	*camino*	*kahmeenoa*
field	*campo*	*kahmpoa*
channel	*canal*	*kahnahl*
canteen	*cantimplora*	*kahnteemplorah*
highway	*carretera*	*kahrraytayrah*
house	*casa*	*kahssah*
hut	*caseta*	*kahsaytah*
sky	*cielo*	*thyayloa*
summit	*cima*	*theemah*
nail	*clavo*	*klahbhoa*
hill	*colina*	*koaleenah*
shell	*concha*	*koanchah*
current	*corriente*	*korryayntay*
rope	*cuerda*	*kwayrdhah*
summit	*cumbre*	*koombray*
rest	*descanso*	*dayskahnsoa*
shower	*ducha*	*doochah*
bay	*ensenada*	*aynsaynahdhah*
reef	*escollo*	*ayskoayoa*
shotgun	*escopeta*	*ayskoapaytah*
stable	*establo*	*aystahbloa*
basin	*estanque*	*aystahnkay*
star	*estrella*	*aystrayyah*
trip	*excursión*	*aykskoorsyon*
lighthouse	*faro*	*fahroa*
float	*flotador*	*floatahdhoar*
fire	*fuego*	*fwaygoa*
fountain	*fuente*	*fwayntay*
rifle	*fusil*	*fooseel*
glasses	*gafas*	*gahfahss*

glacier	glaciar	glahthyahr
gulf	golfo	goalfoa
farm	granja	grahnkhah
grotto	gruta	grootah
ice	hielo	yayloa
immersion	inmersión	eenmayrsyon
insect	insecto	eensayktoa
island	isla	eeslah
lake	lago	lahgoa
lantern	linterna	leentayrnah
plain	llano	yahnoa
spring	manantial	mahnahntyahl
sea	mar	mahr
backpack	mochila	moacheelah
mountain	montaña	moantahñah
swimming	natación	nahtahthyon
snow	nieve	nyaybhay
wave	ola	oalah
landscape	paisaje	pahysahkhay
bird	pájaro	pahkhahroa
view	panorama	pahnorahmah
walk	paseo	pahsayoa
grass	pasto	pahstoa
fisherman	pescador	paydkahdhoar
fish	pez	payth
pick	pico	peekoa
stone	piedra	pyaydrah
pine forest	pinar	peenahr
plant	planta	plahntah
beach	playa	plahyah

grassland	prado	prahdhoa
town	pueblo	pwaybloa
bridge	puente	pwayntay
port	puerto	pwayrtoa
sunset	puesta de sol	pwaystah day soal
racket	raqueta	rahkaytah
flock	rebaño	raybahñoa
refuge	refugio	rayfookhyoa
river	río	reeoa
rock	roca	roakah
lifeboat	salvavidas	sahlbhahbheedhass
forest	selva	saylbhah
path	sendero	sayndhayroa
hedge	seto	saytoa
seat	silla	seeyah
sun	sol	soal
towel	toalla	toahyah
torrent	torrente	torrayntay
springboard	trampolín	trahmpoaleen
lawn chair	trineo	treenayoa
sled	tumbona	toomboanah
vacation, holiday	vacación	bhahkahthyon
barrier	valla	bhahyah
valley	valle	bhahyay
wind	viento	bhyayntoa
vineyard	viñedo	bheeñaydhoa

4. Health

4.1. Medicine

I need to see a doctor.	*Necesito que me vea un médico.*	*naythayseetoa kay may bhayah oon maydeekoa.*
When does the doctor see patients. It's urgent.	*¿A qué hora pasa la consulta el médico? Es urgente.*	*Ah kay oarah pahsah lah konsooltah ayl maydeekoa? Ayss oorkhayntay.*
What symptoms do you have?	*¿Qué síntomas tiene?*	*Kay seentoamahs tyaynay?*
I'm not feeling well.	*No me encuentro bien.*	*Noa may aynkwaytroa byayn.*
I haven't been able to sleep all night.	*No he podido dormir en toda la noche.*	*Noa ay podheedhoa dhoarmeer ayn toadhah lah noachay*
I feel sick, I have a headache, stomach ache, my throat hurts, my ears hurt.	*Tengo ganas de vomitar..., dolor de cabeza, estómago, garganta, oídos.*	*Tayngoa gahnahss day bhoameetahr..., dhoaloar day kahbaythah, aystoamahgoa, gahrgahntah, oaeedoass.*
I'm about to give birth.	*Estoy a punto de dar a luz.*	*Aytoi ah poontoa day dahr ah looth.*

I think I have a fever, indigestion.	*Creo que tengo fiebre, indigestión.*	*Krayoa kay tayngoa fyaybray, eendeekhaystyon.*
Where does it hurt?	*¿Dónde le duele?*	*Doanday lay dwaylay?*
It hurts here, I have ... symptoms.	*Me duele aquí, tengo síntomas de...*	*May dwaylay ahkee, tayngoa seentoamahss day....*
I think I have broken my arm, my ankle.	*Creo que me he roto un brazo, un tobillo.*	*Krayoa kay may ay roatoa oon brahthoa, oon toabeeyoa.*
I feel dizzy.	*Me encuentro mareado.*	*May aynkwaytroa mahrayahdhoa.*
I feel a lot of pressure on my chest.	*Siento una fuerte presión en el pecho.*	*Syayntoa oonah fwayrtay praysyon ayn ayl paychoa.*
He's fallen and hurt his head.	*Se ha caído y está herido en la cabeza.*	*Say ah caheedhoa ee aystah ayreedhoa ayn lah kahbaythah.*
Take your clothes off, raise your sleeve, please.	*Quítese la ropa, súbase la manga, por favor.*	*Keetaysay lah roapah, soobahsay lah mahngah, por fahbhor.*
How often should I take them?	*¿Cada cuánto tiempo debo tomarlas?*	*Kahdhah kwahntoa tyaympoa bayboa toamahrlahss?*

Open your mouth, close your hand, straighten out your body.	*Abra la boca, cierre la mano, estire el cuerpo.*	*ahbrah lah boakah, thyayrray lah mahnoa, aysteeray ayl kwayrpoa.*
Take a deep breath.	*Respire profundo.*	*Rayspeeray proafoondhoa.*
I'm going to give you a shot.	*Le pondré una inyección.*	*Lay pondray oonah eenyaykthyon*
I'm going to take your pressure, temperature.	*Le voy a tomar la tensión, la temperatura.*	*lay bhoay ah toamahr lah taynsyon, lah taympayrahtoorah.*
It's nothing serious, rest a few days and take this medicines.	*No tiene nada grave, descanse unos días y tómese estas medicinas.*	*Noa tyaynay nahdhah grahbhay, dayskahnsay oonoass deeahss ee toamaysay aystahss maydetheenahss.*
Before or after meals, on an empty stomach?	*¿Antes o después de las comidas, en ayunas?*	*Ahntayss oa dayspwayss day lahss komeedahss, ayn ahyoonahss?*
I have had a heart attack, a heart attack, I have been operated in my...	*He tenido un infarto... ataque al corazón, he sido operado de...*	*Ay tayneedhoa oon eenfahrtoa... ahtahkay ahl korahthoan, ay seedhoa apayrahdhoa day....*

I have hypertension, allergies to antibiotics, to penicillin...	*Soy hipertenso, alérgico a los antibióticos, a la penicilina...*	*Soi eepayrtaynsoa, ahlayrkhekoa ah loass ahnteebyoateekoass, ah lah payneetheeleenah...*
We have to bandage your cut, your ankle.	*Tenemos que vendarle la herida..., el tobillo...*	*Taynaymoass kay bhayndahrlay lah ayreedhah..., ayl toabeeyoa.*
I'm pregnant.	*Estoy embarazada.*	*Aystoi aymbahrahthahdhah.*
I need you to check my vision.	*Necesito que me gradúe la vista.*	*Naythayseetoa kay may grahdhway lah bheestah.*
How much do I owe you?	*¿Cuánto le debo?*	*kwahntoa lay dayboa?*
You need to check yourself into a hospital, go to the hospital to have some x-rays taken, check up, analysis.	*Debe usted hospitalizarse, ir al hospital para que le hagan unas radiografías, exploración, análisis.*	*daybay oostayd oaspeetahleethahrsay, eer ahl oaspeetahl pahrah kay lay ahgahn oonahss rahdyoagrahfeeahss, ayksploarahthyon, ahnahleeseess.*
Could you give me local anesthesia?	*¿Puede ponerme anestesia local?*	*Pwayday ponayrmay ahnaystaysyah loakahl?*

You need to have your appendix operated on.	*Debe operarse de apendicitis.*	*Daybay oapayrahrsay day ahpayndeetheeteess*
I have lost my filling.	*He perdido el empaste de una muela.*	*Ay payrdheedhoa ayl aympahstay day oonah mwaylah.*
My teeth hurt very much. do you have an analgesic?	*Me duelen mucho las muelas, ¿tiene un analgésico?*	*May dwahlayn moocho lahss mwaylahss, Tyaynay oon ahnahlkhayseekoa?*
I have to take out a tooth.	*Tengo que sacarle un diente.*	*Tayngoa kay sahkahrlay oon dyayntay.*

Vocabulary

Health

Medicine	*Medicina*	*Medicine*
acidity	*acidez*	*ahtheedhayth*
exhaustion	*agotamiento*	*ahgoatahmyayntoa*
allergy	*alergia*	*ahlayrkhyah*
bladder	*ampolla*	*ahmoayah*
anemia	*anemia*	*ahnaymyah*
anesthesia	*anestesia*	*ahnaystaysyah*
angina	*anginas*	*ahnkheenahss*
appendicitis	*apendicitis*	*ahpáyndeetheetees*
scratch	*arañazo*	*ahrahñahthoa*
arthritis	*artriris*	*ahrtreereess*
asthma	*asma*	*ahsmah*
attack	*ataque*	*ahtahkay*

English	Spanish	Pronunciation
mouth	*boca*	*boakah*
bronchitis	*bronquitis*	*broankeeteess*
cramp	*calambre*	*kahlahmbray*
cancer	*cáncer*	*kahnthayr*
capsule	*cápsula*	*kahpsoolah*
cavities	*caries*	*kahryayss*
cold	*catarro*	*kahtahrroa*
sciatica	*ciática*	*thyahteekah*
colic	*cólico*	*koleekoa*
colitis	*colitis*	*koleeteess*
congestion	*congestión*	*konkhaysthyon*
cut	*corte*	*kortay*
constipated	*constipado*	*konsteepahdhoa*
shock	*choque*	*choakay*
denture	*dentadura*	*dayntahdhoorah*
fainting	*desmayo*	*daysmahyoa*
diabetes	*diabetes*	*dyahbaytayss*
diarrhea	*diarrea*	*dyahrrayah*
tooth	*diente*	*dyayntay*
pain	*dolor*	*doaloar*
gum	*encía*	*ayntheeah*
illness, disease	*enfermedad*	*aynfayrmaydhahdh*
chills	*escalofríos*	*ayskahloafreeoass*
poisoning	*envenenamiento*	*aynbaynaynahmyayntoa*
stinging	*escoriación*	*aysoryahthyon*
enamel	*esmalte*	*aysmahltay*
sneeze	*estornudo*	*aystoarnoodhoa*
stress	*estrés*	*aystayss*
extraction	*extracción*	*aykstrakthyon*
pharingitis	*faringitis*	*fahreengeeteess*

fever	*fiebre*	*fyaybray*
fracture	*fractura*	*frahktoorah*
garglings	*gárgaras*	*gahrgahrahss*
gastritis	*gastritis*	*gahstreeteess*
hematoma	*hematoma*	*aymahtoamah*
wound	*herida*	*ayreedhah*
hernia	*hernia*	*ayrnyah*
indigestion	*indigestión*	*eendeekhaysthyon*
heart attack	*infarto*	*eenfahrtoa*
infection	*infección*	*eenfaykthyon*
inflammation	*inflamación*	*eenflahmahthyon*
heatstroke	*insolación*	*eensoalahthyon*
insomnia	*insomnio*	*eesoamnyoa*
intoxication	*intoxicación*	*eentoakseekahthyon*
headache	*jaqueca*	*khahkaykah*
lesion	*lesión*	*laysyon*
lumbago	*lumbago*	*loombahgoa*
dislocation	*luxación*	*looksahthyon*
sickness	*mareo*	*mahrayoa*
bite	*mordedura*	*moardaydoorah*
molar	*muela*	*mwaylah*
nerve	*nervio*	*nayrbhyoa*
pneumonia	*neumonía*	*naywmoaneeah*
neuralgia	*neuralgia*	*naywrahlkhyah*
sty	*orzuelo*	*oarthwayloa*
ear infection	*otitis*	*oateeteess*
throbs	*palpitaciones*	*pahlpeetahthyonss*
paralysis	*parálisis*	*pahrahleeseess*
peritonitis	*peritonitis*	*payreetoaneeteess*
sting	*picadura*	*peekahdhoorah*

prothesis	*prótesis*	*proatayseess*
puncture	*punzada*	*poonthahdhah*
burn	*quemadura*	*kaymahdhoorah*
root	*raíz*	*raheeth*
cold	*resfriado*	*raysfryahdhoa*
symptoms	*síntomas*	*seentoamahss*
sinuses	*sinusitis*	*seenooseeteess*
tension	*tensión*	*taynsyon*
tetanus	*tétano*	*taytahnoa*
twist	*torcedura*	*toarthaydhoorah*
neck cramp	*tortícolis*	*toarteekoaleess*
cough	*tos*	*toass*
trauma	*traumatismo*	*trahwmahteesmoa*
thrombosis	*trombosis*	*troamboaseess*
tumor	*tumor*	*toomoar*
ulcer	*úlcera*	*oolthayrah*
varicose veins	*varices*	*bhahreethayss*
vertigo	*vértigo*	*bhayrteegoa*
vomit	*vómito*	*bhoameetoa*
Illnesses, diseases	*Enfermedades*	*Illnessess, diseases*
flu	*gripe*	*greepay*
hepatitis	*hepatitis*	*aypahteeteess*
leukemia	*leucemia*	*laywthmyah*
meningitis	*meningitis*	*mayeengeeteess*
poliomyelitis	*poliomielitis*	*polyoamyayleeteess*
measles	*sarampión*	*sahrahmpyoan*
AIDS	*SIDA*	*SEEDHAH*
syphilis	*sífilis*	*seefeeleess*
typhus	*tifus*	*teefooss*

ferina cough	tosferina	toasfayreenah
tuberculosis	tuberculosis	toobayrkooloaseess
chicken pox	varicela	bahreethaylah
pock	viruela	beerwaylah
Hospital	*Hospital*	Hospital
abortion	aborto	ahboartoa
ambulance	ambulancia	ahmboolahnceeah
national health clinic	ambulatorio	ahmboolahtoareeoa
analysis	análisis	ahnahleeseess
antitetanic	antitetánica	ahteetaytahneekah
scalpel	bisturí	beestooree
bed	cama	kahmah
stretcher	camilla	kameeyah
cardiologist	cardiólogo	kardyoaloagoa
surgeon	cirujano	theerookhahnoa
clinic	clínica	thleeneekah
midwife	comadrona	komahdroanah
consultation	consulta	koansooltah
infection	contagio	koantahkhyoa
convalescence	convalecencia	konbahlaythaynthyah
cure	curación	koorahthyon
dermatologist	dermatólogo	dayrmahtoaloagoa
disinfection	desinfección	dayseenfaykthyon
nurse	enfermera	aynfayrmayrah
sick person	enfermo	aynfaymoa
epidemic	epidemia	aypeedaymyah
cast	escayola	aykahyoalah
gynecologist	ginecólogo	kheenaykoaloagoa
intervention	intervención	eentayrbaynthyon

syringe	*jeringuilla*	*khayreengweeyah*
massage	*masaje*	*mahsahkhay*
medication	*medicación*	*maydeekahthyon*
medication	*medicamento*	*maydeekahmayntoa*
medicine	*medicina*	*maydeetheenah*
improvement	*mejora*	*maykhoarah*
opthamologist	*oculista*	*oakooleestah*
operation	*operación*	*oapayrahthyon*
orthopedic	*ortopédico*	*oartoapaydeekoa*
patient	*paciente*	*pahthyaytay*
birth	*parir*	*pahreer*
childbirth	*parto*	*pahrtoa*
pediatrician	*pediatra*	*paydyahtrah*
psychiatrist	*psiquiatra*	*seekyahtrah*
operating room	*quirófano*	*keeroafahnoa*
x-ray	*radiografía*	*rahdyoagrahfeeah*
suture	*sutura*	*sootoorah*
therapy	*terapia*	*tayrahpyah*
thermometer	*termómetro*	*tayrmoamaytroa*
transfusion	*transfusión*	*trahnsfoosyon*
urgency	*urgencia*	*oorkhaynyah*
urologist	*urólogo*	*ooroaloagoa*
vaccine	*vacuna*	*bahkoonah*

4.2. Pharmacy

Where can I find a chemist ?	*¿Dónde puedo encontrar una farmacia?*	*Doanday pwaydhoa aynkontrahr oonah fahrmahthyah*

I would like some pills for a cough...	*Quisiera unas pastillas para la tos...*	*Keeyayrah oonahss pahsteeyahss pahrah lah toass...*
Could you give me a shot?	*¿Podrían ponerme una inyección intramuscular?*	*Podreeahn ponayrmay oonah eenyaykthyon eentrahmooskoolahr?*
We can't give you this drug without a prescription.	*No le podemos servir este medicamento sin receta médica.*	*Noa lay podaymoass sayrbeer aystay maydeekahmayntoa seen raythaytha maydeekah.*
do I need a prescription for this drug?	*¿Necesito receta para adquirir esta medicina?*	*Naythayseetoa raythaytah pahrah ahdhkeereer aystah maydeetheenah?*

Vocabulary

distilled water	*agua destilada*	*ahgwah daysteelahdhah*
oxygenated water	*agua oxigenada*	*ahgwah oakseekhaynahdhah*
needle	*aguja*	*ahgookhah*
alcohol	*alcohol*	*ahlkoaoal*
analgesic	*analgésico*	*ahnahlkhayseekoa*
anti-acid	*antiácido*	*ahtyahtheedhoa*
antibiotic	*antibiótico*	*ahteebhyoateekoa*
contraceptive	*anticonceptivos*	*ahteekoanthaypteeboass*
antidote	*antídoto*	*ahteedhoatoa*
aspirin	*aspirina*	*ahspeereenah*

bicarbonate	bicarbonato	beekahrboanahtoa
sedative	calmante	kahlmahntay
capsule	cápsula	kahpsoolah
healing	cicatrizante	theekahtreethahntay
compresses	compresas	komprayshass
tablet	comprimido	kompreemeedhoa
dropper	cuentagotas	kwayntahgoatahss
sucker	chupete	choopaytay
disinfectant	desinfectante	dayseenfayktahn
band-aid	esparadrapo	ayspahrahdhrahpoa
sterile	estéril	aystayreel
chemist	farmacéutico	fahrmahthaywteekoa
chemist	farmacia	fahrmahthyah
gauze	gasa	gahsah
drops	gotas	goatahss
insulin	insulina	eensooleenah
injection	inyección	eenyaykthyon
syrup	jarabe	khahrahbay
syringe	jeringuilla	khayreengweeyah
laxative	laxante	lahksahntay
diapers	pañales	pahñahlayss
handkerchiefs	pañuelos	pahñwayloass
pap	papilla	pahpeeyah
pill	píldora	peeldhoarah
cream	pomada	poamahdhah
preservatives	preservativos	praysayrbhahteebhoass
prescription	receta	raythaytah
sedative	sedante	saydhahntay
sleeping pill	somnífero	soamneefayroa
suppository	supositorio	soopoaseetoaryoa

tampons	*tampones*	*tahmpoanayss*
tranquilizer	*tranquilizante*	*trahnkeeleethahntay*
vaseline	*vaselina*	*bahsayleenah*
bandage	*venda*	*bayndhah*
vitamins	*vitaminas*	*beetahmeenahss*
iodine	*yodo*	*yoadoa*

4.3 The human body

tonsils	*amígdalas*	*ahmeegdhahlahss*
appendix	*apéndice*	*ahpayndeethay*
artery	*arteria*	*ahrtayryah*
articulation	*articulación*	*ahrteekoolahthyon*
armpit	*axila*	*ahkseelah*
belly	*barriga*	*bahrreegah*
spleen	*bazo*	*bahthoa*
mouth	*boca*	*boakah*
arm	*brazo*	*brahoa*
head	*cabeza*	*kahbaythah*
hip	*cadera*	*kadhayrah*
face	*cara*	*kahrah*
brow	*ceja*	*thaykhah*
brain	*cerebro*	*thayraybroa*
elbow	*codo*	*koadoa*
spine	*columna vertebral*	*koaloomnah bhayrtaybrahl*
heart	*corazón*	*koarahthoan*
rib	*costilla*	*koasteelyah*
cranium	*cráneo*	*krahnayoa*
neck	*cuello*	*kwayyoa*
body	*cuerpo*	*kwayrpoa*

Health

finger	*dedo*	*daydhoa*
diaphragm	*diafragma*	*dhyahfrahgmah*
tooth	*diente*	*deeayntay*
duodenum	*duodeno*	*dwoadaynoa*
gum	*encía*	*ayntheeah*
esophagus	*esófago*	*aysoafahgoa*
back	*espalda*	*ayspahldah*
breastbone	*esternón*	*aystayrnoan*
stomach	*estómago*	*aystoamahgoa*
femur	*fémur*	*faymoor*
forehead	*frente*	*frayntay*
throat	*garganta*	*gahrgahntah*
gland	*glándula*	*glahndhoolah*
liver	*hígado*	*eegahdhoa*
shoulder	*hombro*	*oambroa*
bone	*hueso*	*wayssoa*
bowel	*intestinos*	*eetaysteenoass*
lip	*labio*	*lahbhyoa*
tongue	*lengua*	*layngwah*
jaw	*mandíbula*	*mahndeebhoolah*
hand	*mano*	*mahnoa*
chin	*mejilla*	*maykheeyah*
cheek	*mentón*	*mayntoan*
wrist	*muñeca*	*mooñaykah*
muscle	*músculo*	*mooskooloa*
thigh	*muslo*	*moosloa*
buttock	*nalga*	*nahlgah*
nose	*nariz*	*nahreeth*
nerve	*nervio*	*nayrbhyoa*
nape	*nuca*	*nookah*

eye	ojo	oakhoa
navel	ombligo	oambleegoa
ear	oreja	oakraykhah
genitals	órganos genitales	oargahnoass khayneetahlayss
ovary	ovario	oabhahryoa
palate	paladar	pahlahdahr
calf	pantorrilla	pahntoareeyah
chest	pecho	paychoa
hair	pelo	payloa
penis	pene	paynay
nípol	pezón	paythoan
foot	pie	pyay
skin	piel	pyayl
leg	pierna	pyayrnah
lung	pulmón	poolmoan
kidney	riñón	reeñoan
knee	rodilla	roadheeyah
blood	sangre	sahgray
breast	seno	saynoa
nervous system	sistema nervioso	seestaymah nayrbhyoasoa
armpit	sobaco	soabahthoa
ankle	talón	tahloan
tendon	tendón	tayndoan
tibia	tibia	teebhyah
thorax	tórax	toarahks
windpipe	tráquea	trahkayah
fingernail	uña	ooñah
vagina	vagina	bahkheenah

bladder	*vejiga*	*baykheegah*
vein	*vena*	*baynah*
vertebra	*vértebra*	*bayrtaybrah*
Fingers	*Dedos*	*Fingers*
ring	*anular*	*ahnoolahr*
middle	*corazón*	*koarahthoan*
index	*índice*	*eendeethay*
pinky	*meñique*	*mayneekay*
thumb	*pulgar*	*poolgahr*

5. Time

5.1. Days, weeks, months, calendar

I like the mountains most in the winter.	*En invierno es cuando más me gusta la montaña.*	*Ayn eenbhyayrnoa ayss kwahndoa mahss may goostah lah moantahñah.*
What day is today?	*¿Qué día es hoy?*	*Kay deeah ayss oi?*
We will leave for the beach July fifth.	*Nos marcharemos el 5 de julio a la playa.*	*Noass mahrchahraymoass ayl (5) theekoa day khoolyoa ah lah plahyah*
What year did you say you were born?	*¿En qué año has dicho que naciste?*	*Ayn kay ahñoa ahss deechoa kay nahtheestay?*
In nineteen eighty-three.	*En 1983.*	*Ayn meel noabhay theeayntoass oachayntah ee trayss (1983)*

How old is your father?	¿Cuántos años tiene tu padre?	*Kwahntoas ahñoass tyaynay too pahdhray?*
He is sixty-three years old.	Tiene 63 años.	*Tyaynay saysayntah ee trayss (63) ahñoass.*
Next autumn, I would like to go to Paris.	En el próximo otoño quisiera ir a París.	*Ayn ayl proakseemoa oatoañoa keesyayrah eer ah Pahreess*
We leave for holiday in three days.	Dentro de tres días salimos de vacaciones de verano.	*Dayntroa day trayss deeahss sahleemoass day bhahkahthyonss day bhayrahnoa.*
We have an appointment for the dentist next Tuesday at ten a.m.	El próximo martes tenemos cita a las diez de la mañana con el dentista.	*Ayl proakseemoa mahrtayss taynaymoass theetah ah lahss dyayth day lah mahñahnah kon ayl daynteestah.*
Spring starts in a month.	Dentro de un mes se inicia la primavera.	*Dayntroa day oon mayss say eeneethyah lah preemahbhayrah.*
Tomorrow Sunday, mid afternoon, we'll go to the cinema.	Mañana domingo, a media tarde, iremos al cine.	*Mahñahnah dhoameengoa, ah maydyah tahrday, eeraymoass ahl theenay.*
Next year, my birthday is on a Wednesday.	El año que viene, mi cumpleaños cae en miércoles.	*Ayl ahñoa kay bhyaynay, mee koomplayahñoass kahay ayn myayrkoalayss.*

I started skiing in the eighty's.	*Yo comencé a esquiar en los años 80.*	*Yo komaynthay ah ayskeeahr ayn loass ahñoas oachayntah (80)*
Tuesday the thirteenth, like tomorrow, is my lucky day.	*Los martes día trece, como mañana, me dan siempre suerte.*	*Loass mahrtayss deeah traythay, koamoa mahñahnah, may dahn syaympray swayrtay.*
We are almost at the end of the twentieth century.	*Ya estamos a finales del siglo XX.*	*Yah aystahmoass ah feenahlayss dayl seegloa bhayntay (XX)*
Next Thursday, I have ticketsfor the theatre.	*El próximo jueves tengo unas entradas para el teatro.*	*Ayl prokseemoa khwaybhayss tayngoa oonahss ayntrahdhahss pahrah ayl tayahtroa.*

Vocabulary

day	*día*	*deeah*
dawn	*amanecer*	*ahmahnaythayr*
early morning	*de madrugada*	*day mahdhroogahdhah*
day before yesterday	*antes de ayer*	*ahntayss day ahyayr*
yesterday	*ayer*	*ahyayr*
the eve	*la víspera*	*lah bheespayrah*
today	*hoy*	*oi*
tomorrow	*mañana*	*mahñahnah*
day after tomorrow	*pasado mañana*	*pahsahdhoa mahñahnah*
in the morning	*por la mañana*	*por lah mahñahnah*

Time

noon	*mediodía*	*maydyoadeeah*
afternoon	*tarde*	*tahrday*
dusk	*atardecer*	*ahtahrdaythayr*
twilight	*crepúsculo*	*kraypooskooloa*
night	*noche*	*noachay*
midnight	*medianoche*	*maydyahnoachay*
Week	*Semana*	*Week*
monday	*lunes*	*loonayss*
tuesday	*martes*	*mahrtayss*
wednesday	*miércoles*	*myayrkolayss*
thursday	*jueves*	*khwaybhayss*
friday	*viernes*	*bhyaynayss*
saturday	*sábado*	*sahbahdhoa*
Sunday	*domingo*	*doameengoa*
Months	*Meses*	*Months*
january	*enero*	*aynayroa*
february	*febrero*	*faybrayroa*
march	*marzo*	*mahrthoa*
april	*abril*	*ahbreell*
may	*mayo*	*mahyoa*
june	*junio*	*khoonyoa*
july	*julio*	*khoolyoa*
august	*agosto*	*ahgoastoa*
september	*septiembre*	*sayptyaymbray*
october	*octubre*	*oaktoobray*
november	*noviembre*	*nobhyaymbray*
december	*diciembre*	*deethyaymbray*
month	*mes*	*mayss*
bimester	*bimestre*	*beemaystray*
trimester	*trimestre*	*treemaystray*
semester	*semestre*	*saymaystray*

Time

Seasons	Estaciones del año	Seasons
spring	*primavera*	*preemahbhayrah*
summer	*verano*	*bhayrahnoa*
autumn	*otoño*	*oatoañoa*
winter	*invierno*	*eenbhyayrnoa*
leap year	*año bisiesto*	*ahñoa beesyaystoa*
biennium	*bienio*	*byaynyoa*
quintennium	*quinquenio*	*keenkaynyoa*
decade	*década*	*daykahdhah*
century	*siglo*	*seegloa*
millennium	*milenio*	*meelaynyoa*
ages	*época*	*aypoakah*
Era	*Edades*	**Era**
old age	*antigua*	*ahnteegwah*
middle ages	*media*	*maydyah*
modern age	*moderna*	*moadayrnah*
contemporary	*contemporánea*	*kontaympoarahnayah*
Adverbs	Adverbios	*Adverbs*
often	*a menudo*	*ah maynoodhoa*
sometimes	*a veces*	*ah bhaythayss*
now	*ahora*	*ahoarah*
yet	*aún*	*ahoon*
quickly	*de prisa*	*day preesah*
hardly ever	*de tarde en tarde*	*day tahrday ayn tahrday*
at some time	*alguna vez*	*ahlgoona bhayth*
from time to time	*de vez en cuando*	*day bhayth ayn kwahndoa*
then	*luego*	*lwaygoa*
later	*después*	*dayspwayss*

Time

right away	*enseguida*	*aynsaygeedhah*
meantime	*entretanto*	*ayntraytahntoa*
meanwhile	*mientras tanto*	*myayntrahss tahntoa*
a while ago	*hace tiempo*	*ahthay tyaympoa*
immediately	*inmediatamente*	*eenmaydyahtahmayntay*
never	*jamás*	*khahmahss*
never	*nunca*	*noonkah*
soon	*pronto*	*proantoa*
rarely	*raramente*	*rahrahmayntay*
always	*siempre*	*syaympray*
yet	*todavía*	*toadhahbheeah*
already	*ya*	*yah*

5.2. Climate and temperature

It's a sunny day.	*Hace un día soleado.*	*Ahthay oon deeah soalayahdhoa*
It's cloudy, it will probably rain.	*Está nublado, es probable que llueva.*	*Aystah nooblahdhoa, ayss proabahblay kay ywaybhah.*
Well, as long as it stays like this, we'll have a lot of snow.	*Pues, como sigamos así podremos tener una gran nevada.*	*Pwayss, koamoa seegahmoass ahsee podraymoass taynayr oonah grahn naybhahdhah.*
Do you think it will be cold, hot where we are going?	*¿Cree que hará mucho frío, calor, donde vamos?*	*Kray kay ahrah moochoa freeioa, kahloar, doanday bhahmoass?*

I have opened the windows and it's very sunny.	*He abierto las ventanas y hace un sol estupendo.*	*Ay ahbyayrtoa lahss bhayntahnahss ee ahthay oon soal aystoopayndhoa.*
I think that today it will be cold, and it will rain.	*Creo que hoy, además de hacer frío, va a llover.*	*Krayoa kay oi, ahdhaymahss day ahthayr freeoa, bhah ah yoabhayr.*
The weather forecast said it would be one degree below zero.	*El parte meteorológico indica que hará un grado bajo cero.*	*Ay pahrtay maytayoaroaloakheek oa endeekah kay ahrah oon grahdhoa bahkhoa thayroa*
What will the weather be like tomorrow?	*¿Qué temperatura puede hacer mañana?*	*Kay taympayrahtoorah pwayday ahthayr mahñahnah?*

Vocabulary

cloudburst	*aguacero*	*ahgwahthayroa*
air	*aire*	*ahyray*
atmosphere	*atmósfera*	*ahtmoasfayrah*
barometer	*barómetro*	*bahromaytroa*
downpour	*bochorno*	*boachoarnoa*
heat	*calor*	*kahloar*
climatic	*climático*	*kleemahteekoa*
climatology	*climatología*	*kleemahtoaloakheeah*
showers	*chubascos*	*choobahskoass*
frost	*escarcha*	*ayskahrchah*

Time

star	estrella	aystrayyah
cold	frío	freeoa
hailstorm	granizada	grahneethahdhah
hail	granizo	grahneethoa
frozen	helado	aylahdhoa
ice	hielo	yayloa
humidity	humedad	oomaydhahdh
hurricane	huracán	oorahkahn
rain	lluvia	yoobhyah
fog	niebla	nyayblah
snow	nieve	nyaybhay
cloud	nube	noobay
raingage	pluviómetro	ploobhyoamaytroa
ray	rayo	rahyoa
lightning	relámpago	raylahmpahgoa
dew	rocío	roathyoa
sun	sol	soal
shade	sombra	soambrah
temperature	temperatura	taympayrahtoorah
storm	tormenta	toarmayntah
thunder	trueno	trwaynoa
wind	viento	bhyayntoa
Sky	*Cielo*	*Sky*
overcast	cubierto	koobyayrtoa
clear	despejado	daypaykhahdhoa
overcast	encapotado	aynkahpoatahdhoa
starry	estrellado	aystrayahdhoa
gray	gris	greess
cloudy	nuboso	nooboasoa
sunny	soleado	soalayahdhoa

Climate	Clima	Climate
continental	*continental*	*konteenayntahl*
humid	*húmedo*	*oomaydhoa*
rainy	*lluvioso*	*yoobhyoasoa*
mediterranean	*mediterráneo*	*maydeeayrrahnayoa*
polar	*polar*	*poalahr*
dry	*seco*	*saykoa*
temperate	*templado*	*taymplahdhoa*
tropical	*tropical*	*troapeekahl*

5.3. Time

What time do you have, please?, what time is it, please?	*¿Qué hora tiene usted, por favor?*	*Kay oarah tyaynay oostaydh por fahbhor?*
It's quarter to eleven, twenty to, ten to, five to.	*Son las once menos cuarto, menos veinte, menos diez, menos cinco minutos.*	*Soan lahss oanthay maynoass kwahtroa, maynoass bhayntay, maynoass dyayth, maynoass theenkoa meenootoass.*
The metro comes every three minutes.	*El metro pasa cada tres minutos.*	*Ayl maytroa pahsah kahdhah trayss meenootoass.*
When should we meet?	*¿A qué hora quedamos?*	*Ah kay oarah kaydhahmoass?*

In about seven minutes, in a little bit, in less than half an hour.	*Dentro de siete minutos, dentro de un rato, menos de media hora.*	*Dayntroa day syaytay meenootoass, dayntroa day oon rahtoa, maynoass day maydyah oarah.*
It's eleven o'clock, quarter past eleven, eleven thirty, eleven forty-five.	*Son las once en punto, y cuarto, y media, y tres cuartos.*	*Soan lahss oanthay ayn poontoa, ee kwahrtoa, ee maydyah, ee trayss kwahrtoass.*
It's almost eleven.	*Son casi las once.*	*Soan kahsee lahss oanthay.*
In an hour I'll be there.	*En una hora estoy contigo.*	*Ayn oonah oarah aytoi konteegoa.*
It's eleven five, ten, fifteen, twenty, twenty-five, thirty, thirty-five, forty, forty-five, fifty, fifty-five.	*Son las once y cinco, diez, quince, veinte, veinticinco, treinta, treinta y cinco, cuarenta, cuarenta y cinco, cincuenta, cincuenta y cinco minutos.*	*Soan lahss oanthay ee theenkoa, dyayth, keenthay, bhayntay, bhayntaytheenkoa, trayntah, trayntah ee theenkoa, kwahrayntah, kwahrayntah ee theenkoa, theenkwayntah, theenkwayntah ee theenkoa meenootoass.*
How long before it's finished?	*¿Dentro de cuánto tiempo estará acabado?*	*Dayntroa day kwahntoa tyaympoa aystahrah ahkahbahdhoa?*

second	*segundo*	*saygoondhoa*
minute	*minuto*	*meenootoa*
hour	*hora*	*oarah*
quarter of an hour	*un cuarto de hora*	*oon kwahrtoa day oarah*
half hour	*media hora*	*maydyah oarah*
three quarters of an hour	*tres cuartos de hora*	*trayss kwahrtoass day oarah*
it's in the morning	*es por la mañana*	*ayss por lah mahñahnah*
at night	*de noche*	*day noachay*
in the middle of the day, midday	*a mediodía*	*a maydyahdeeah*
in the afternoon	*por la tarde*	*por lah noachay*
midnight	*medianoche*	*maydyahnoachay*
early in the morning	*madrugada*	*mahdhroogahdhah*

6. Communication

6.1. Telephone

What area code do I need to call...?	*¿Qué prefijo debo marcar para llamar a...?*	*Kay prayfeekhoa dayboa mahrkahr pahrah yahmahr ah...?*
Where is there a public phone?	*¿Dónde hay un teléfono público?*	*Doanday ay oon taylayfoanoa poobleekoa?*

How does this phone work?	¿Cómo funciona este teléfono?	Koamoa foonthyoanah aystay taylayfoanoa?
What number should I dial?	¿Qué número debo marcar?	Kay noomayroa dayboa mahkahr?
Operator, please connect me to room two thirteen, with extension fifteen.	Operadora, póngame con la habitación número 213, con la extensión 15.	Oapayrahdhoarah, poangahmay kon lah ahbeetahthyon noomayroa doass oonoa trayss (213), kon lah aykstaynsyon keenthay (15)
You have the wrong number, this isn't it.	Se ha confundido de número telefónico, aquí no es.	Say ah konfoondheedhoa day moomayroa taylayfoaneekoa, ahkee noa ayss.
May I ask who is calling?	¿De parte de quién?	Day pahrtay day kyayn?
Will it take long to connect me to the embassy?	¿Tardará mucho en poder comunicar con la embajada?	Tahrdhahrah moochoa ayn podhayr komooneekahr kon lah aymbahkhahdhah?
Will you pay for the call or is it collect?	¿La llamada telefónica la abona usted o es a cobro revertido?	Lah yahmahdhah taylayfoaneekah lah ahboanah oostaydh oa ayss ah koabroa raybhayrteedhoa?

Please wait a minute, don't hang up, hold the line	*Espere un momento, por favor, no cuelgue.*	*Ayspayray oon moamayntoa, por fahbhor, noa kwaylgway.*
Could you speak more slowly, please?	*¿Puede hablar más despacio, por favor?*	*Pwayday ahblahr mahss dayspahthyoa, por fahbhor?*
He's not here right now, could you call later? He is not in	*No está en este momento, ¿podría llamar más tarde?*	*Noa aystah ayn aystay moamayntoa, podreeah yahmahr mahss tahrday?*
You could call in fifteen minutes.	*Puede usted llamar dentro de quince minutos.*	*Pwayday oostaydh yahmahr dayntroa day keenthay meenootoass.*
No answer.	*No contesta.*	*Noa kontaystah.*
My phone number is...	*Mi número de teléfono es...*	*Mee noomayroa day taylayfoanoa ayss...*
Good morning, I would like to speak to information.	*Buenos días, quisiera hablar con la oficina de información.*	*Bwaynoass deeahss, keeyayrah ahblahr kon lah oafeetheenah day eenfoarmahthyon.*
It's connected.	*La línea telefónica está comunicando.*	*Lah leenayah taylayfoaneekah aystah komooneekahndhoa.*

Communication

Vocabulary

telephone	*aparato telefónico*	*ahpahrahtoa taylayfoaneekoa*
public telephone	*teléfono público*	*taylayfoanoa poobleekoa*
tókens	*de fichas*	*day feechahss*
card	*de tarjeta*	*day tahrkhaytah*
switchboard	*centralita*	*thaytrahleetah*
headphone	*auricular*	*ahwreekoolahr*
mobile	*móvil*	*moabheel*
take off the hook	*descolgar*	*dayskoalgahr*
dial	*marcar*	*mahrkahr*
phone guide	*guía telefónica*	*geeah taylayfoaneekah*
booth	*cabina*	*kahbeenah*
conference	*conferencia*	*konfayraythyah*
operator	*operadora*	*oapayrahdhoarah*
fax	*fax*	*fahks*

6.2. Correspondence and the post office

Where is the post office, please?	*¿Dónde está la oficina de correos, por favor?*	*Doanday aystah lah oafeetheenah day korrayoass, por fahbhor?*
Would you give me postage for this envelope, package?	*¿Querría franquearme este sobre, paquete?*	*Kayrreeah frahnkayahrmay aystay soabray, pahkaytay?*
Where is the mailbox?	*¿Dónde está el buzón?*	*Doanday aystah ayl boothoan?*

I would like to send this letter certified and next day (urgent), how much is it?	*Deseo enviar esta carta certificada y urgente, ¿cuánto cuesta?*	*Daysayoa aynbhyahr aystah kahrtah thayrteefeekahdhdhah ee oorkhayntay, kwahntoa kwaystah?*
What window do I need to buy stamps, send certified mail?	*¿Dónde está la ventanilla de los sellos, certificados?*	*Doanday aystah lah bhayntahneeyah day loass sayyoass, thayrteefeekahdhoass?*
I would like to send a telegram, where is the telegraph office?	*Deseo poner un telegrama, ¿dónde está el servicio de telégrafos?*	*Daysayoa ponayr oon taylaygrahmah, doanday aystah ayl sayrbheethyoa day taylaygrahfoass?*
I would like to send a telegram, how much do you charge per word?	*Deseo poner un telegrama, ¿cuánto cobran por palabra?*	*Daysayoa ponayr oon taylaygrahmah, kwahntoa kobrahn por pahlahbrah?*
I'm here to pick up a money order, telegram.	*Vengo a recoger un giro postal, telegráfico.*	*Bhayngoa ah raykoakhayr oon kheeroa poastahl, taylaygrahfeekoa.*
Is there a letter, telegram in my name?	*¿Hay alguna carta, giro, telegrama a mi nombre?*	*Ay ahlgoonah kahrtah, kheeroa, taylaygrahmah ah mee noambray?*

Communication

post office box	apartado de correos	ahpahrtahdhoa day korrayoass
mailbox	buzón	boothoan
letter	carta	kahrtah
certified letter	carta certificada	kahrtah thayrteefeekahdhah
mail carrier	cartero	kahrtayroa
communication	comunicación	komooneekahthyon
mail	correo	korrayoa
correspondence	correspondencia	korrayspoandaynthyah
addressee	destinatario	dayteenahtahryoa
returning	devolver	daybhoalbhayr
refund	devolución	daybhoaloothyon
address	dirección	deeraykthyon
shipping	envío	aynbheeoa
date	fecha	faychah
postage	franqueo	frahnkayoa
money order	giro postal	kheeroa poastahl
printed	impreso	eempraysoa
tax	impuesto	eempwaystao
mailing list	lista de correos	leestah day korrayoass
sample	muestra sin valor	mwaystrah seen bhahloar
stamped paper	papel sellado	pahpayl sayyahdhoa
mailed package	paquete postal	pahkaytay poastahl
weight	peso	paysoa
postcard	postal	poastahl

receipt	*recibo*	*raytheeboa*
remittent	*remitente*	*raymeetayntay*
stamp	*sello*	*sayyoa*
envelope	*sobre*	*soabray*
rate	*tarifa*	*tahreefah*
telefax	*telefax*	*taylayfahks*
telegraph	*telégrafo*	*taylaygrahfoa*
telegram	*telegrama*	*taylaygrahmah*
urgent	*urgente*	*oorkhayntay*
window	*ventanilla*	*bhayntahneeyah*

6.3. Colors

| What color is the...? | ¿De qué color es...? | *Day kay koloar ayss...?* |

Vocabulary

yellow	amarillo	*ahmahreeyoa*
blue	azul	*ahthool*
navy blue	azul marino	*ahthool mahreenoa*
beige	beige	*baykhay*
white	blanco	*blahnkoa*
chestnut	castaño	*kahstahñoa*
color	color	*koloar*
colored	coloreado	*koloarayahdhoa*
flat color	color liso	*koloar leesoa*
striped	colores a rayas	*koloarayss ah rahyahss*
florescent	fosforescente	*foasforaysthayntay*
gray	gris	*greess*
lilac	lila	*leelah*

185

brown	marrón	*mahrroan*
chrome	metalizado	*maytahleethahdhoa*
purple	morado	*morahdhoa*
brown	moreno	*moraynoa*
orange	naranja	*nahrahnkhah*
black	negro	*naygroa*
red	rojo	*roakhoa*
pink	rosa	*roasah*
blond	rubio	*roobyoa*
green	verde	*bhayrday*
violet	violeta	*bhyoalaytah*

6.4. Numbers and measurements

6.4.1 Numbers

Vocabulariy		
Cardinal	*Cardinales*	Cardinal
zero	*cero*	*thayroa*
one	*uno*	*oonao*
two	*dos*	*doass*
three	*tres*	*trayss*
four	*cuatro*	*kwahtroa*
five	*cinco*	*theenkoa*
six	*seis*	*sayss*
seven	*siete*	*syaytay*
eight	*ocho*	*oachoa*
nine	*nueve*	*nwaybhay*
ten	*diez*	*dyaayth*
eleven	*once*	*oantay*
twelve	*doce*	*doathay*
thirteen	*trece*	*traythay*

fourteen	*catorce*	*kahtorthay*
fifteen	*quince*	*keenthay*
sixteen	*dieciséis*	*dyaytheesayss*
seventeen	*diecisiete*	*dyaythesyaytay*
eighteen	*dieciocho*	*dyaytheeoachoa*
nineteen	*diecinueve*	*dyaytheenwaybhay*
twenty	*veinte*	*bhayntay*
thirty	*treinta*	*trayntah*
forty	*cuarenta*	*kwahrayntah*
fifty	*cincuenta*	*theenkwayntah*
sixty	*sesenta*	*saysayntah*
seventy	*setenta*	*saytayntah*
eighty	*ochenta*	*oachayntah*
ninety	*noventa*	*noabhayntah*
hundred	*cien*	*thyayn*
two hundred	*doscientos*	*doassthyayntoass*
three hundred	*trescientos*	*tayssthyayntoass*
four hundred	*cuatrocientos*	*kwahtroathayayntoass*
five hundred	*quinientos*	*keenyayntoass*
six hundred	*seiscientos*	*saysthyayntoass*
seven hundred	*setecientos*	*saytaythyayntoass*
eight hundred	*ochocientos*	*oachoathyayntoass*
nine hundred	*novecientos*	*noabhaythyayntoass*
thousand	*mil*	*meel*
million	*millón*	*meeyoan*

Ordinals	*Ordinales*	*Ordinals*
first	*primero*	*preemayroa*
second	*segundo*	*saygoondoa*
third	*tercero*	*tayrthayroa*
fourth	*cuarto*	*kwahrtoa*

fifth	quinto	*keentoa*
sixth	sexto	*saykstoa*
seventh	séptimo	*saypteemoa*
eighth	octavo	*oaktahbhoa*
ninth	noveno	*noabhaynoa*
tenth	décimo	*daytheemoa*
eleventh	undécimo	*oondaytheem*
twelfth	duodécimo	*dwoadaytheemoa*
thirteenth	decimotercero	*daytheemoatayrthayroa*
fourteenth	decimocuarto	*daytheemoakwahrtoa*
fifteenth	decimoquinto	*daytheemoakeentoa*
sixteenth	decimosexto	*daytheemoasaykstoa*
seventeenth	decimoséptimo	*daythemoasaypteemoa*
eighteenth	decimoctavo	*daytheemoaktahbhoa*
nineteenth	decimonoveno	*daytheemoanoabhaynoa*
twentieth	vigésimo	*bheekhayseemoa*
thirtieth	trigésimo	*treekhayseemoa*
fortieth	cuadragésimo	*kwahdrahkhayseemoa*
fiftieth	quincuagésimo	*keenkwahkhayseemoa*
sixtieth	sexagésimo	*sayksahkhayseemoa*
seventieth	septuagésimo	*sayptwahkhayseemoa*
eightieth	octogésimo	*oaktoakhayseemoa*
ninetieth	nonagésimo	*noanahkhayseemoa*
hundredth	centésimo	*thayntayseemoa*

Fractions	Fracciones	Fractions
zero point five	0´5 cero coma cinco	*thayroa koamah theenkoa*
two point fifty	2´50 dos coma cincuenta	*doass koamah theenkwayntah*
thirty five percent	35 % treinta y cinco por ciento	*trayntah ee theenkoa por thayayntoa*

one half	*1/2 un medio*	*oon maydyoa*
one third	*1/3 un tercio*	*oon tayrthyoa*
two fourths	*2/4 dos cuartos*	*doass kwahrtoass*
three fifths	*3/5 tres quintos*	*trayss keentoass*
two sixths	*2/6 dos sextos*	*doass saykstoass*
one tenth	*1/10 un décimo*	*oon daytheemoa*
figure	*cifra*	*theefrah*
addition	*suma*	*soomah*
subtraction	*resta*	*raystah*
multiplication	*multiplicación*	*moolteepleekahthyon*
division	*división*	*deebheesyon*
double	*doble*	*doablay*
triple	*triple*	*treeplay*
cuadruple	*cuádruple*	*kwahdrooplay*
five times	*quíntuple*	*keentooplay*
half	*mitad*	*meetahdh*
one time	*una vez*	*oonah bhayth*
three times	*tres veces*	*trayss bhaythayss*
even	*par*	*pahr*
uneven	*impar*	*eempahr*
pair	*pareja*	*pahraykhah*
dozen	*docena*	*doathaynah*
dozen and half	*docena y media*	*doathaynah ee maydyah*
two weeks	*quincena*	*keenthaynah*
hundred	*centenar*	*thayntaynahr*
percentage	*porcentaje*	*porthayntahkahy*

6.4.2. Measurements

The country road is wider after the fifteenth kilometer.	*La carretera comarcal es más ancha a partir del kilómetro 15.*	*Lah kahrraytayrah koamahrkahl ayss mahss ahnchah ah pahrteer dayl keeloamaytroa keenthay (15)*
This frame measures three by nine metres.	*Este cuadro mide 3 por 9 metros.*	*Aystay kwahdroa meedhay trayss por nwaybhay maytroass*
How much does this cheese weigh?	*¿Cuánto pesa este queso?*	*Kwahntoa paysah aystay kaysoa?*
Give me a kilo and a half of fillets.	*Déme kilo y medio de filetes.*	*Daymay keeloa ee maydyoa day feelaytayss*
Give me three quarters of a kilo of ham.	*Déme tres cuartos de kilo de jamón.*	*Daymay trayss kwahrtoass day keeloa day khahmoan*
What is the area of this piece of land?	*¿Cuál es la superficie de esta parcela?*	*Kwahl ayss lah soopayrfeethyay day aystah pahrthaylah?*
What does this door measure?	*¿Cuánto mide esta puerta?*	*Kwahntoa meehay aystah pwayrtah*
How deep is this gallery?	*¿Qué profundidad tiene esta galería?*	*Kay proafoodheedhahdh tyaynay aystah gahlayreeah?*

How much can this container hol?	¿Qué capacidad tiene este recipiente?	Kay kahpahtheedhahdh tyaynay aystay raytheepyayntay?

Vocabulary

Weight	Peso	Weight
gram	gramos	grahmoass
fifty grams	cincuenta gramos	theenkwayntah grahmoass
half a kilo	medio kilo	maydyoa keeloa
three quarters of a kilo	tres cuartos de kilo	trayss kwahrtoass day keeloa
hundredweight	quintal	keentahl
ton	tonelada	toanaylahdhah
net weight	peso neto	paysoa naytoa
gross weight	peso bruto	paysoa brootoa
hangup	tara	tahrah
Longitude	**Longitud**	*Longitude*
millimeter	milímetro	meeleemaytroa
centimeter	centímetro	thaynteemaytroa
decimeter	decímetro	daytheemaytroa
meter	metro	maytroa
kilometer	kilómetro	keeloamaytroa
mile	milla	meeyah
height	altura	ahltoorah
width	anchura	ahnchoorah
thickness	grosor	groasoar
depth	profundidad	proafoondheedhahdh

Communication

Surface and volume	Superficie y volumen	Superficie and volumen
square centimeter	cm² centímetro cuadrado	thaynteemaytroa kwahdhrahdhoa
square meter	m² metro cuadrado	maytroa kwahdhrahdhoa t
cubic centimeter	cm³ centímetro cúbico	haynteemaytroa koobeekoa
cubic meter	m³ metro cúbico	maytro koobeekoa
area	área	ahrayah
hectare	hectárea	aytahrayah
square kilometer	km² kilómetro cuadrado	keeloamaytroa kwahdhrahdhoa

Capacity	Capacidad	Capacity
quarter of a liter	cuarto de litro	kwahrtoa day leetroa
half a liter	medio litro	maydyoa leetroa
liter	litro	leetroa
hectalitre	hectolitro	ayktoaleetroa.